Vie

Kelly Melang, Author

**ISBN-13:
978-1983837685**

**ISBN-10:
1983837687**

TABLE OF CONTENTS

DEDICATION

This book is dedicated to my family.
Jeff, Wolf and Max, who put up with the hours involved in
writing this book.

ACKNOWLEDGMENTS

Sometimes you arrive at a crossroads in your life, my choice was either go up or down. I chose to go up.

This book is dedicated to Beech Mountain Parkway, the road from Banner Elk to Beech Mountain. I've navigated you during snow, ice, fog, even torrential downpours. To the wildlife saying hello along the way, even those jumping in front of my car on a dark winter night.

You've made driving fun as I navigate the same curves that scared the crap out of me that first drive.

I'm glad when I was traveling through Banner Elk, I followed the sign for "Beech Mountain," ignoring the "Snow and Ice on the Road Use 4 Wheel Drive" lights flashing and drove up.

Here's to many more stories.

INTRODUCTION

Well Hello!
Aren't you cold?

It's 14 degrees outside, come in and sit by the fire. I just made a pot of coffee, would you like a cup? Whether you are coming to visit us for the first time, or here year after year, this book is intended to explain some of the curious occurrences along with letting you in a little lore, while providing tidbits for a relaxing and enjoyable stay.

I began my story on Beech Mountain as a tourist, driving the two hours from Winston Salem in search of snow, as well as traveling in the summer to escape the 95 degrees/100 percent humidity of the lowlands. My weekend jaunts moved into full summers on Beech, the magic of this mountain taking over. I homeschooled my children one year, gaining more time on the mountain during snow season, edging closer to my goal of changing my address permanently. After our year of homeschool, we all decided that experiment didn't work out. I was lucky enough my children love the mountain as much as I do, with agreement from everyone we became full time residents.

There's a great book about Beech Mountain, written by Arcadia Publishing, giving you all the historical information. The reason Beech Mountain has tourists is its elevation. At 5506 above sea level, Beech Mountain is the highest incorporated town in Eastern America with temperatures during the summer rarely breaking 80 degrees and an average snowfall during winter time of 84 inches. What I intend to do is fill in that history with tips, tidbits and stories of the mountain. There is an ongoing saying on the mountain, good advice for anyone new to the top, "What happens on the mountain, stays on the Mountain."

Is your coffee hot enough? Good. OK, let's begin.

Let's Start With The Basics of 36.206374, -81.883115

Beech Mountain is Eastern America's Highest Incorporated town east of the Rockies sitting 5506 feet above sea level.

With a permanent population of 375 residents (of which we are three of them), the town accommodates over 10,000 new residents and visitors during the winter season and over 5,000 during the summer season.

Beech Mountain is located in both Avery and Watauga Counties, the US Census stating the town occupying 6.7 square miles.

As of this printing there are 2,350 dwellings on the mountain, the median home price over 300,000.

The town of Beech Mountain started as a resort town in the 1960s, when Beech Mountain Resort was created by Grover Robbins of Blowing Rock, NC. Originally, the Robbins brothers, along with 40 other investors developed Beech Mountain along with other resorts, as part of the Carolina Caribbean Corporation. The Corporation went bankrupt in the 1970's after building the ski resort, town roads and utility system. The home owners association, collecting fees for the corporation, took control of the recreation, water and maintenance systems. In 1977, the Beech Mountain Utility System, a subsidiary of the property owner's association, purchased the water and sewer systems from the courts, creating the Sanitary District in 1980 bringing all utilities under one roof.

In 1981, the town of Beech Mountain is incorporated by the North Carolina General Assembly.

A few facts about Beech Mountain Resort courtesy of
www.beechmountainresort.com

Opened 1967, Beech Mountain resort is the highest ski resort in Eastern America
8 lifts, 17 trails
98 skiable acres
Base 4675' Peak 5506'
Vertical - 830 feet
Lift capacity - 10,258 per hour.
Snowmaking available for 100% coverage
Ice skating
Tubing Park
Two Terrain Parks
Four Restaurants
Two sports shops
Full rental equipment

Summertime downhill mountain bike park with
3 Easy runs
3 More Difficult runs
2 Very Difficult runs
2 Extremely Difficult runs
2 Beginner Skills Areas

20 miles of hiking trails

50 miles of paved cycling routes

Emerald Outback Bike Trails - 8 miles of beginning to challenging bike/hike trails.

Bark Park

Two Lakes, Buckeye Lake and Coffey Lake

Buckeye Recreation Center

Beech Mountain Club

Sledding Hill

Beech Mountain Brewery

10 Restaurants

3 Beech Mountain Club Restaurants

Stocked and Wild Fishing Rivers

1. PROTECT THAT BIGGEST ASSET!

I need to start off with the most important part of your arsenal on Beech Mountain, all seasons! Sunscreen! Why wear sunscreen?

Sunscreen does two things, while reflecting the sun's rays away from the body, other compounds absorb the sun's rays protecting the skin.

Why am I taking the time here talking specifically about sunscreen? Because no matter the season, sunscreen is your most important weapon to protect your greatest asset. Did you know that close to 20 square feet of skin covers your body? Your skin is your largest organ.

Skin consists of three layers: the epidermis, the outermost layer of skin, providing the waterproof covering for our body (though some beg to differ on a rainy day) also determining your skin tone. The dermis is the next layer containing tough connective tissue, hair follicles and sweat glands (blame that for the foul odor during the summer). Last, the deeper subcutaneous tissue holding fat and connective tissue. I think my subcutaneous tissue is on over drive right now. Put away the Ben and Jerrys!

You skin color, or tanning color comes from melanocytes in the skin. When the sun hits the epidermis, it naturally produces melanocytes as protection, thus turning your skin brown. So technically, any type of color to your skin is sun damage.

As you enjoy the cooler temperatures of higher altitudes, keep in mind the higher you go, the less filters to the sun's rays, meaning in layman's terms - the sun is more intense. This gives you a better chance of burning. Constant burning on the skin can cause irreparable damage (google Tan Woman if you want a scare) it can also lead to skin cancer.

One of most susceptible times to sun burn is usually the first warm days of spring. On Beech Mountain, this usually doesn't happen until mid-June. This is the time you need to be mindful of the sunscreen. Those lily white legs of winter have been hidden for months behind the long underwear, the snow pants and the jeans. Just like the little tiny animals peeking from their hollows in the woods, you must take care with that vampire skin. Put your sunscreen on early and develop a base color, then enjoy the days of spring and summer without a burn. I've always thought people working outdoors are some of the healthiest people. They don't use as much sunscreen as most people do - a little Vitamin D goes a long way.

Another time to watch your skin is during our beautiful blue bird days of winter, days when the temperature soars to a balmy 26 degrees, the sun is shining, the snow is fresh. Many, excited to get their first tracks on the mountain, forget the sunscreen on their face. This leads to goggle burn, a beautiful red color to your cheeks on a winter day coupled with a nice white outline where your goggles sat for the day. During the summer with sun glasses, this is called "raccoon eyes." Living on a mountain, goggle tan is considered sexy. If you are a visitor, you may have some explaining to do to friends and family when you return home, especially if you purchase some kind of funky shaped goggles.

So, how do sunscreens work? The SPF of sunscreen is the Sun Protection Factor or protection against UV radiation, called UVB. Think of the B as in burning because this radiation causes sun burn and several types of skin cancer. Most dermatologists recommend a sunscreen with an SPF of between 15 and 50, anything over 50 does not provide any more protection. The SPF of 15 and 50 both protect 97% of the UVB rays from your skin. That's as high as it goes folks. Currently you cannot find sunscreen protecting 100% of the UVB rays.

So how does the SPF number work? This number reflects how long it will take before your skin turns red. For example, with an SPF of 15 if you are fair skinned and it takes ten minutes in the sun for your skin to burn, you are extending this 15 times or roughly 150 minutes or 2.5 hours. Since fun in the sun usually involves swimming or sweating, the American Cancer Society always recommends reapplying sunscreen inside this window, or for fair skin very often. The only thing better than sunscreen on a sunny Beech Mountain day is completely covering your skin with a hat, sunglasses, long sleeves and pants. I'll leave that up to you.

Last but not least, when protecting your skin, don't forget your eyes. A good pair of goggles in the winter, sunglasses in the summertime. Sunburnt eyes tend to be red, itchy and dry after exposure, taking 2-3 days to return to normal. Like sunburnt skin, repeated sunburnt eyes can result in cloudy vision. I never go out without eye protection, sunglasses for the sun, or goggles for the sun and the blowing snow of winter. An eyeful of snow does not feel good.

I'm dedicating a whole chapter to sun protection because being closer to the sun can feel like being closer to heaven, but a really bad sunburn can feel like hell.

2. SHE'LL BE COMING AROUND THE MOUNTAIN

One of the benefits of living on top of a mountain is the cooler temperatures during the summer along with the potential of snowfall during the winter. One usually thinks the quickest way of getting from PointA to PointB is a straight line, but this is not true when it comes to climbing a mountain in a car. Beech Mountain Parkway, (aka Highway 184) is a windy road starting down in Banner Elk (some T-shirts boast it is a "drinking town with a skiing problem") ending at Beech Mountain town hall located at 5049 above sea level. This road is full of switchbacks usually making a first time driver up or down the mountain very nervous.

Summertime driving tips: During the summer, Beech Mountain grows from 350 residents to over 5,000 residents as Floridians relocate escape the heat of summertime in Florida. During the summer, the speed limit of Beech Mountain Parkway changes due to several reasons. Some like driving the 3.3 miles so they can see the sights, others enjoy 22 MPH because that is the fastest their car will go. Still others drive slowly because they enjoy pissing off the people trailing behind them. If you end up in the 8-15 car line following the one car driving 13 miles per hour, the best thing to do is turn the radio up, roll down your windows on a summer day, and relax. Everyone else sitting in that line feels your pain.

If you are a slow driver, or behind a slow driver traveling up the mountain, there are two opportunities on Beech Mountain Parkway for passing. You'll know these when the road increases to two lanes. The problem with both of them is that they are on a pretty good incline on the mountain, meaning opportunity is short. The first is about three quarters of a mile up Beech Mountain Parkway on a steep incline. If you are a stick shift or manual drive, get ready by putting your car in lower gear before the passing lane. If you are the slow driver in the front of the line, when the road opens up, move to the right and slow down. This does not mean stay in the left lane making sure no one passes you (unless you are in the "let's get everyone pissed off" mode.) The people who know how to drive this mountain will zip past you, leaving behind the cars perfectly content with 13 miles per hour. Pat yourself on the back for doing your good deed for the day. Or do what a few residents do, travel like a slug to the top of the mountain, finally pulling over at Brick Oven Pizza, giving everyone the finger as they pass you!

Coming Down The Mountain. If you are driving down the mountain and smell something burning, that's someone's brakes. They are doing what we call, "laying on them" or riding the brake all the way down the mountain. I once saw smoke coming out from an Impala ahead of me going down Beech Mountain Parkway. This is not only bad for your brakes, but irritates everyone behind you as they roll up their windows, getting away from the smell. Take the advice on a sign as you leave Beech Mountain, "Gear Down For Safety." This means, put your car in a lower gear allowing the slowing motion of the gears to slow you down, not the foot laying on the brake. Your car's brakes and everyone around you will thank you for gearing down the mountain.

Who has the right of way on Beech Mountain? There are many different ways of determining the right of way. First, the senior citizen, they've been around much longer than you. Second, the deer because they will stand in the middle of the road staring at you like "What?". Third, a skunk because it is not easy getting that smell off the tires of your car. Fourth, the Bear because they are usually dragging a trash can with them and it could damage your car. Basically, everyone except you. Keep this rule in mind and enjoy our seldom "rush minute" on the mountain as drivers wait for wildlife to cross the road.

Wintertime Tips - the same road, Highway 184 changes completely when it comes to winter on Beech Mountain. The cold temperatures create a kind of weather havoc on roads. First rule of thumb, whether you are visiting or living on the mountain is to check your tires before the start of winter season. Are they good snow tires? How old are they? Do they still have a good tread? If you are not sure about your tires, have your local mechanic check them out. Remember, if you go to the tire store inquiring whether you need new tires, you know the answer. If you are just visiting, and do not have winter tires, plan on purchasing tire chains for winter travel. These can be found on websites or inquiring with your local mechanic. There are several places in Banner Elk providing tire chains and installation prior to climbing Beech Mountain. Tire chains basically, attach to the outside of your tire, adding grip helping you get through icy and snowy roads.

Make sure you don't become the butt of any jokes on Beech Mountain. Remember if you have a rear wheel drive car, the chains go on the rear wheels. They will not do you any good on the front wheels. They are supposed to provide the traction. Also, the chains go on when the roads are snow covered, putting them on your car when the roads are dry ensures sparks flying out from your tires while driving, locals pointing and laughing, and possible damage to your tires.

Fill your tank with gas BEFORE climbing the mountain as we do not have a gas station at the top. You do not want to get stuck by the side of a slippery road overnight, watching your 1/4 tank dwindle down to nothing. Everything takes longer when navigating slippery roads so have enough gas getting you to where you are going.

With ABS brakes, the pumping of the brakes on slick roads is done by the car, not by you. ABS brakes start when the driver hits the brake, the car pumping the brakes, slowly stopping the car. If one wheel locks in a skid, it lets the brake off on that wheel, pumping the others until the skidding tire finds grip for stopping. This feature helps with braking, but also slows the braking process, meaning you should allow much longer distances between you and the driver ahead of you when driving on slick roads with ABS brakes.

The car kit. Any resident of a town prone to winter weather understands the winter car kit. Some are basic, other's preparing for Armageddon with what they keep in their trunk. A basic car kit includes a blanket, jug of water, protein bars, flashlight, gloves, hand warmers and kitty litter. No, I'm not talking about bringing a cat with you, the kitty litter provides traction if you get stuck and your wheels are spinning. If the kitty litter doesn't work, many keep a baseball bat or 2x4 for better traction. Place the baseball bat or 2x4 in front of or behind the wheel, as the wheel turns, the length of the wood, lifts it out of the rut dug by spinning the wheels in snow or mud. Also, keep a good piece of rope, some recommend the extra large dog leash or horse lead in the trunk, in case a good samaritan stops and is willing to pull you out of a ditch. This could save you the fees from the wrecker.

Why have a car kit? This past winter a friend was traveling up the backside of Beech Mountain on 194. He noticed tire tracks going from the road over the side into a ditch. On a whim, he decided to check it out, finding a truck sitting a few feet down the ditch crashed into the trees. Climbing down, he found a man sitting in the front seat of the car. The guy opened his eyes saying, "Man I am glad you found me. I've been sitting here for two days." Two days! Of course he was a good old boy from TN, used to our weather so the only thing he wanted was a sip of water. You never know, better to be safe then sorry.

Driving 101 Snow covered roads mean different driving skills. A few basic pointers, don't slam on your brakes, even if you are sliding. This will increase your slide. Gently pump your brakes, while saying your Hail Marys, hoping the tires find grip. If you start sliding, turn the wheel in the direction of the sliding rear wheels, while saying your Hail Marys. Turning the wheel in the opposite direction could cause the car to spin and possibly overturn.

Look up the number of your local wrecker service, and program it in your phone. If you are new to driving in the snow as I was when I first came up Beech Mountain you will probably find a ditch somewhere. In fact, I think I paid for High South Wrecker Service's first child's college education my first year on the mountain, I even put them on retainer.

Snowplowing. Beech Mountain is very proactive about clearing the roads during the winter time. Plows start immediately with the snow fall, their first priority to clear Beech Mountain Parkway, the main artery of the mountain. If you are on a backroad, you may not see the plow until the next morning. Food for thought, with 2-3 inches of fresh snow, it is easier to navigate the roads before the snowplow comes through or after they throw gravel on the roads. In between is packed down slippery snow. If you are shoveling your driveway, start at the top because starting at the bottom ensures the plow coming by and covering up all your work. You can also look up several local landscapers and put them on retainer for snow plowing in the winter. Who needs the entire driveway plowed when your car stays at the bottom of driveway anyway? One resident with an extremely long steep driveway, gave up the plowing and purchased a snowmobile for taking groceries from the bottom to her kitchen door. Another rigged a cart with a pulley, attached to an old lawn mower motor, pulling the groceries up their driveway.

As you can see, being in a winter wonderland means having to navigate the beautiful snow. Be prepared. Make your vacation enjoyable with the proper planning. Oh, and by the way, don't forget to stop by Fred's General Mercantile for those things you forgot prior to navigating back roads to your home.

Are you cold? It's 14 degrees outside, come in and sit by the fire. I just made a pot of coffee, would you like a cup? Whether you are coming to visit us for the first time, or year after year, this book is intended to explain some of the curious occurrences, while providing tidbits for a relaxing and enjoyable stay. At 5506 above sea level, Beech Mountain is the highest town in Eastern America with temperatures during the summer rarely breaking 80 degrees and an average snowfall during winter of 84 inches. What I intend to do is fill in that history with tips, tidbits and stories of the mountain. There is an ongoing saying on the mountain, good advice for anyone new to the top, "What happens on the mountain, stays on the Mountain." Is your coffee hot enough? Good. OK, let's begin.

3. HOW NOT TO DRIVE IN THE SNOW

With all the snow we received the past few days, I thought I'd share some things NOT to do when dealing with our winter weather.

1. Make sure you leave all the snow piled on top of your car and on the hood. This makes the driver behind you feel like they are in a snow globe as it blows off your car on the road. On another note it will keep drivers behind you at a safe distance.

2. Create a real video game atmosphere by only clearing a 4 in circle on your windshield. This will make you feel like you are in a real M1A1 tank! Bring a toy gun with you to complete the experience.

3. Your hazard lights are a great way to alert all the drivers around you that it is snowing. Make sure they pay attention to you by honking your horn as they pass you.

4. The "I'm about to crap myself" look on your face is great for sagging skin. It will make you look 10 years younger. It is especially flattering when framed by the 4in hole you cleared on your windshield.

5. Your high beams at night are the perfect way to see every snowflake. Turn them on and leave them on for the rest of your vacation.

6. If you have 4WD, even if you've never used it before, make sure you drive as fast as you can, alerting all the other drivers that you have 4WD. This is especially true if you don't know how to turn on your 4WD, drive as fast as you can, your car will let you know when it needs it by sliding into the ditch.

7. The driver in front of you is the perfect leader on the road. Follow that driver as close as you can finding their tracks in the snow. Their hazard lights will let you know when to stop.

8. Check the brakes on your car frequently. Make sure they are in working order by slamming on them when you hit 15 MPH and you were planning on 10 MPH.

9. Your turn begins the second you hit your destined road, don't inconvenience the drivers behind you by slowing down for your turn. Turn signals are not needed as your hazard lights are already on.

10. Make sure you honk hello to the fellow drivers, especially those that do not know they are facing the wrong way on the road or the ones in the ditch. It makes them feel part of the community.

4. DON'T LIKE THE WEATHER? WAIT 15 MINUTES!

"Don't knock the weather. Nine-tenths of the people couldn't start a conversation if it didn't change once in a while." -Ken Hubbard

On Beech Mountain, regardless of the season, the weather is the number one topic of conversation. If you are single and looking to find a good mountain girl, take the time to study the weather. It will not only give you something to talk about, but might impress that possible mate. If you can't find anything in common, the easiest thing to focus on is the weather.

Summertime weather borders on rainforest. You'll see a beautiful sunny day, plan your hike, get halfway through it when a single cloud passes over and the heavens open up. If I am taking a back pack on a hike, I always throw in a poncho or raincoat, If you don't have one just go ahead and throw a trash bag in there, just don't put it over your head unless it has a hole, or you could suffocate (legalese told me to include that warning, guess Darwin is still at work.) Better yet, like every permanent resident, just enjoy the rainy hike, they are the ones from which stories are made.

Summers are one of the reasons so many flock to Beech Mountain. Starting in June, the temperature never really goes above 80 degrees. Since 90% of our summertime visitors are from Florida, sunny and 70 degrees sounds so much better than South Miami Beach in August. The sun will make it feel warmer. Rather than retreating to air conditioning, park under the shade of an umbrella, tree or other cover and you'll see what makes Beech Mountain famous, beautiful skies and cooler temperatures. Beech Mountain Club has an offer during the summer, if the temperature hits over 80 degrees during June, July or August, your round of golf is free. Typically that is when you'll see locals in the loin cloths, because to us 80 degrees is Africa hot!

Ray's Weather Center, a local website offers daily forecasts with a "Golf-O-Meter" telling you the beauty of the day in 1-5 golf balls, 5 being best. In the spring, the Golfball-O-Meter changes to a "Raccoon-O-Meter" for the week of MerleFest, a major music festival in Wilkesboro, NC, a tribute to Doc and Merle Watson. The raccoon is the mascot of Merle's band, "Frosty Morn" and, after a naming contest was called Flat Top, which is fitting since Merle and Doc were both masters of the Flat Top guitar. 5 raccoons tell you the day is spectacular, 1 raccoon means there's a lot of rain in the forecast.

Towards the end of summer, all the full timers on the mountain start talking about and studying the upcoming winter. Those that live through winters on the mountain take our weather very seriously. Sure we look at all the obvious indicators: websites and the NOAA, then we start looking at the mountain lore. Two major weather indicators on Beech Mountain are August fogs,(locals say a good August fog means a good winter snow event. Many put a bean in a jar with each fog, counting them at the end of month as part of their winter plans. Of course us snow enthusiasts are looking for a FULL jar, but we'll take whatever we can get. Another is the birthing of animals, if the deer and other residents on the mountain have their offspring early, it is a good sign for a snowy winter If the birthing is late, it could be a mild winter. On the mountain, size does matter, if the animals are small during the summer, this means a harsh winter. Weather predictions change from the front side to the back side of

Beech Mountain, from the old timers to the newcomers with their computer models. Your best bet? Research your own weather and stick to that.

Of course the biggest source of predicting winter weather is the Wooly Worm. The town of Banner Elk holds a Wooly Worm Festival in October. The Wooly Worm is the brown and black caterpillar found in the High Country. People come from far and wide to race worms up a string, the fastest worm winning a cash prize and the privilege of predicting the weather for winter. Races run in heats throughout the day on Saturday and Sunday, the winner declared Saturday night, Sunday heats mainly for fun. The rings on the worm are measured as the weeks of winter, mostly brown meaning mild, mostly black means snowy. I once raced Wooly Worms with my boys. Unfortunately, I dropped Steve our caterpillar on the ground right before the race. Perhaps that was why he kept going DOWN the string rather than racing to the top. My son said he was confused. No one can accurately predict the weather, but as I mentioned before it is always the source of many a good conversation.

Wintertime weather watching is a hobby of most residents of Beech Mountain, mainly because venturing out onto the roads without a quick check of the weather could have your car in a ditch, or worst yet, overnighting in the cold waiting on a wrecker. Parents on Beech Mountain monitor the weather the minute it starts threatening, hoping for the "morning where everyone can sleep in," or a snow day. Some complain the High Country of North Carolina has too many snow days but the biggest thing to remember is many students come from the tops of mountains, or single lane valley roads to school. When determining a snow day, your road may seem passable, but somewhere out there are rural roads making administrators thinking about teens new to driving, uncomfortable enough to close school for the day. Good news about snow days is the ski resorts offer discounts to local students. If it is going to snow, might as well enjoy it. Visit websites for discount options at local resorts.

There are many different websites determining winter weather. There is an ongoing debate on the mountain about Ray's Weather Center and Todd's Weather. I always check both when making my daily plans. One thing I do like about Ray's Weather is the "SnowMan-O-Meter." A pile of water means no chance, while a full snowman you can barely see means blizzard type conditions. There is nothing more exciting than seeing the red banner at the top of Ray's indicating Severe Weather Alert. Everyone's sleeping in the next day!

Major weather websites indicate they cover Beech Mountain weather, but be careful as sometimes they are recording conditions in Banner Elk, not on Beech Mountain. 5506 degrees above sea level makes a big difference. I've always said, "If you don't like the weather on Beech Mountain, then drive down to Banner Elk." Some days it is literally blizzard conditions on the mountain top but rain in Banner Elk. If you are unsure of the weather, there are many different webcams giving you a real time view. You can visit Beech Mountain Resort's website webcams, several of the local hotels including Beech Alpen Inn Webcams, and High Country webcams. If you pull up the Town Hall webcam and cannot see the road due to snow, then rethink plans if you are driving up that night, (see Snow Driving 101) or make sure you have your car kit. Oh, and if you are visiting get all your errands in before driving to your cabin, back roads are usually worse than main roads.

Another strange weather event on Beech Mountain is the temperature inversion. On most days, temperatures drop as you travel higher in elevation. Most of the sun's energy is converted to heat at the ground level, the warm air rises, and the higher it goes the more it cools down. On a temperature inversion, the warmer air does not move as quickly away from ground level. Usually cloud cover, frozen ground and a few other factors create this. This basically means you could see above freezing temperatures at 5506' on Beech Mountain, while things are below freezing in Boone. For those of us waiting on snow guns, or Mother Nature, these can be a little frustrating in the winter time.

A big winter factor on Beech Mountain is the wind chill. Many a day on the mountain, Ray's Weather Center will mention it is "Not a day for top hats or toupees," meaning batten down the hatches. Gusts of wind on the mountain can top 60 knots, and that wind can wreak havoc on staying warm. Wind moving over the body increases the rate of heat loss, meaning the temperature on a windy day can feel much cooler than a calm day. Wind chills are calculated with a combination of wind speed and temperature for the wind chill factor. Sometime if you see a wind chill of -14 degrees, you may want to rethink that trip to the slopes, or if you are going, add several extra layers of clothing. If the wind chill factor looks extreme, remember covering every exposed part of your body from the elements is essential, not only because of the heat loss but because of the possibility of frostbite. Ski masks are not just for burglars!

You have your basics about the weather on Beech Mountain, from how cool August Fogs have everyone clapping their hands, to the people waddling around looking like the StayPuff Marshmallow man after reading about the wind chill factor. There's plenty of conversation starters here, along with suggestions on staying comfortable regardless of the temperature.

5. TYPICAL SOUTHERN SNOW

How visitors to Beech Mountain react to a snow event:

If we get snow:

The call for Armageddon will hit Facebook two to three days before the actual arrival of snow.

The bread is gone from the grocery store shelves 15 minutes after the debut of the forecast.

The beer disappears even quicker.

The forecast then changes and everyone is stuck with way too much bread.   You can never have enough beer.

What falls down is more like snizzle - drizzle with a little mixture of snow.

If there is any sign of white on any road surface, traffic in town comes to a complete halt. Luckily there's plenty of beer in the trunk of your car, so you don't panic.

Those that didn't head the calls on Facebook for Armageddon are left to buying the Hard Tack Biscuits because all the bread is gone. Worst yet, they are stuck with Bud Light Lime because all the other beer is gone as well.

What is your plan of attack if there is a threat of snow and you're visiting Beech Mountain?

1. PANIC, then talk amongst your friends on Facebook about how much you do not like snow.

2. DRIVE POORLY - especially when trying to get to the grocery store to get beer and bread.

3. STOCK UP - Our ABC stores are government owned - stock up early in case they are closed.

4. SHUT DOWN EVERYTHING - because no one is going out in the snow, they've stocked up on beer and liquor and are busy on the computer talking about the snow on Facebook.

5. WINTERIZE - I read somewhere that alcohol is a good winterizer, it doesn't freeze as quickly.

6. WEATHER EXPERTS

Did you know there 1,487 weather websites on the web?

Yes, I know because I've checked all of them looking for that pretty little snowflake.

And I am not alone. You'll find in the winter time, everyone becomes an expert at weather.

Chairlift conversations:

"Snow looks good this morning."

That's because adding the Dew point and the temperature = A

then if:-
If A > 7 prob. very little snow
If A=7 prob. snow = 10%
A=6 20%
A=5 30%
A=4 40%
A=3 50%
A=2 60%
A=1 70%
A=0 80% or more."

"Wow, who are you? AccuWeather?"
"No, I'm just a season pass holder."

After hearing my explanation of the weather to someone else on the list, a very nice man asks, "So if it starts raining at 10:45a then we just go to the bar at 5506, is that too early?" All of us, "No!"

Then my lowland friends start texting me, "Is there still snow?"

Of course there is! Don't you check Weather.com or Weather.org or Averyweather.com High Country Web Cams or KellysWebCam.com

Of course I am amazed at our snowmaking capability so I reply with a two page text:

We did have 16 days of non snowmaking weather but our base was good so we are a step ahead. Snowmaking weather returns on Wed night at 1:37am with snowmaking temps through early next week. Thanks to Snomax, a bacteria that keeps the snow from melting as quickly, you should see premium conditions for your visit."

Of course they text back, "Thank you spokesperson for Beech Mountain Resort, I was just asking if I could crash on your couch."

The best is when winter weather approaches, all of us Moms start watching the websites, discussing in texts:

What are you thinking 2 hour delay?
Hell no, 4 inches of snow, we'll get a SNOW DAY! YEAH!
I don't know, the la Nina is separated but not divorced yet from El Nino so could be rain.
No, the latest model has the Polar Vortex dating La Nina and El Nino is pissed of so we'll have snow!
I'm not sure, the Canadian Malamute is sniffing around the Upper Low and with Tropical Storm Lady Gaga's Dance

Partner cheating with La Nina and El Nino having no idea it could mean everything misses us and we get a

Blue Bird Day!

The day arrives and it starts with clouds:

"I told you so, La Nina has more money in the bank than El Nino!" Someone texts!

Then the rain comes and there's more frowny faces flying along the cell phone lines.

Until

It turns to snow.

"I told you so, you should follow (insert weather website here).com," I get in 15 separate texts.

I hold my tongue because my barometric pressure charts along with the dew point calculations and the dance I did naked on my back deck last night only means one thing......

Snow.

7. DO THESE BOOTS MAKE MY BUTT LOOK BIG?
OR, MAKING NEW OLD FRIENDS

During the winter season, dressing appropriately is your key to fun and success on the ski slopes. I always tell my children, "There is no such thing as being cold, only inappropriate clothing." This is especially true when you see a young girl in the tight blue jeans, tank top and high heels on a 14 degree day in December, trying to look sexy as she is shivering to death. Believe me, blue is not a preferred color for your lips.

How do you keep warm on a cold winter day? If you can, stay under the blankets, turn off the alarm clock and roll over to your sweetie. But I digress. The key to warmth above 5506 feet in elevation is layers. It is easier to peel a layer if you find you are over dressed than sitting on the ski lift, realizing the pain of frozen nipples is a distraction. Here's a basic introduction to layering for warmth:

Base layers should always be thin, form fitting (not just to make your better half happy) and moisture wicking. This holds heat to your body while taking the moisture of sweat moving it to the outside of the layer where it evaporates without chilling your skin. Some of my favorite base layers are made of wool or silk, cotton tends to hold moisture so not a very good choice.

First layer is another thin, but less tight layer. A good light fleece or wool sweater is a great choice. This is one of your shed-able layers in case you over dressed. Beech Mountain Resort has a locker system you can rent by the day or year.

Outer layers should always be waterproof. You could be the best skier on the mountain and never fall, but you may sit in a pile of snow or ice on the lift ride to the top. Waterproofing is a necessity. Many learn this quickly after pulling out their 1970's one piece suit, figuring it would work for another year, opening the front door, stepping outside then quickly back inside every pore of the body screaming, "What were you thinking?" Most new equipment already has water proofing. Remember, do not wash it with usual laundry detergent as this will mess up your water proofing seal. Purchase waterproof wash at a local outfitter or just wash with water. If you are purchasing outer wear, plan on a slight size larger, as your base layers underneath will add extra padding. Don't worry, it is normal to have a large booty when on the mountain, it is padding for warmth and, in case we fall.

Don't forget a hat as most body heat leaves through the head. Better yet, think also about a good helmet if you are on the snow, not because of your skill level but because that brand new skier who decided to go to the top, is currently barreling down the slope right behind you. Add in a neck warmer or head scarf, covering exposed parts of your face from the machines blowing snow on the slopes. A good warm set of gloves keep your hands happy, better yet think about a thin pair of gloves under a thick pair of waterproof gloves on your hands. Googles should complete your outfit for protection from the sun and blowing snow.

Once you have the art of dressing for warmth down to a science, the "bluebird day" comes along. A day where Beech Mountain goes from -14 wind chill, to a Carolina blue sky, the sun shining, warming you out of several layers of winter clothes. Since we are closer to the sun, the heat is more intense, making skiers feel warmer while increasing the chances of sunburn. On bluebird days, you can ditch the puffy coat, throw on a lined hoodie and get away with fun on the slopes. I always over dress because sometimes a blue bird day can be very sly - a brilliant, sunny day but with a stiff breeze making you long for the winter coat you left at home. Beech Mountain Ski Resort offers yearly locker services, a wonderful place to store extra layers accessible in case the sun disappears behind a cloud causing a quick dip in the temperature.

Once summertime hits the mountain, we find many of our new friends are actually our old friends on the mountain. Standing outside for a summer concert on the lawn of Beech Alpen or Fred's General Mercantile, we strike up a conversation with someone new, asking all the usual questions. After fifteen minutes of thinking, "I remember someone saying that same thing" we look at that person and realize - we already know them. Old friends become new friends because no one recognizes each other after shedding 15 layers of winter. So if you visit in the winter, then come back in the summer don't be offended if your favorite waiter doesn't recognize you. You have some color to your skin not the vampire white of winter, your hair is natural not plastered to head from a hat, and they can actually see your eyes without the goggles.

Pretty much all seasons on Beech Mountain call for layers. Our spring season is full of surprises with some late May ice or snow storms while the summer has many 50 degree cool nights. Come fall, a 60 degree day can be followed by snow flurries that night. If you are a fan of winter boots or slippers, don't put them away when winter ends, they will come in handy during some Spring and a couple summer days when you'll love wiggling your toes in their warmth. Don't forget a jacket where ever you go, an extra layer in case it gets cold, or a rain jacket for weather changes. If planning an outside garden party, BBQ or going to a concert, that extra blanket you pack may come in handy.

A year round resident is the perfect weather gauge for summertime clothing. Rule of thumb, if you are from further south and see:
Year Rounder wearing pants - put on your parka.
Year Rounder in shorts - pants and sweater are a good bet
Year Rounder in a loin cloth - you can safely wear your shorts that day.

Many summer time residents travel to our neck of the woods from Florida. During the summer, cowboy boots are a natural accessory up here, they sure do look cool, but it is also a great way of covering exposed skin on a cool night.

If you are planning on hiking on Beech Mountain remember your hiking boots. Like putting the wrong tires on a car during winter season, not having the appropriate footwear can make a hike pretty miserable. Many local outfitters in the area sell hiking sandals, my favorite accessory, with the coolness of sandals but the grip of hiking boots. Flip flops in a mountain environment are asking for trouble.

You don't have to worry about high heels and sheer dresses when visiting Beech Mountain, unless you want to. Local residents know that cooler temperatures along with rain, snow, ice or snizzle (snow type drizzle) make dressing comfortably and appropriately the best way to enjoy a vacation.

.

8. HONEY, YOU'RE ON MOUNTAIN TIME

You know it is a good vacation when time stands still, finding those moments you wish would never end. Luckily when arriving at the top of Beech Mountain, you officially enter "Mountain Time," and in some instances time really does stand still.

Can I go back to driving up the mountain again? If you are not behind the Senior Citizen going 13 miles per hour, then usually it is a local, because living up high means you enter the time warp of Mountain Time, where things literally do move at the pace of a tree growing.

Thinking about getting home repair done at your home? On Mountain Time, plan on adding at least 1 hour to 1 week for the repairman. Sometimes we call the repairman, "Mystery Men" because they take the call, line up the job then disappear off the face of the Earth. Don't worry, it's not you, it's where you live. Once the repairman realizes completing the job of clearing your drain requires a drive up Beech Mountain Parkway behind the Senior Citizens in the summer, or the ice and snow of winter, somehow the work ticket blows off the dash of his pickup truck, forgotten forever.

When you do find someone willing to travel up the mountain for repair work, be patient. He usually makes it up Beech Mountain Parkway stopping at Fred's General Mercantile for a quick bite or a soda along the way. There he runs into Ray, who he hasn't seen in two days. They spend thirty minutes or so catching up on Ray, Ray's Mom, Shirley, Ray's two kids Shelly and Earl. Finally, the repairman pats Ray on the back, looking at his watching, saying, "I've got to get going, I've got a job."

Of course leaving Fred's General Mercantile for his car, he runs into Charlie, who he hasn't seen in a few hours. Charlie is another repairman actually completing his job. They chat for another half an hour about Charlie's job before he looks at his watch again. He leaves Fred's General Mercantile, finally, remembering he still has some trash in his car, so plans a quick stop at the dump. Knowing several others at the dump, he spends a few minutes accepting an invitation to dinner, picking up a second job after yours, making a date.

Once he arrives at your house, Mountain Time slows even more. He'll look at your problem. Not for a short time, but long enough for you to actually feel your body aging. He is assessing the problem. Assessing means you will stand next to him quietly, listening to him say, "well" and "oh my," making you think rather than clearing a clog, the house is about to be condemned. After thirty minutes of looking at it, not talking to you, he'll usually turn saying, "OK, looks like an easy fix. Let me get my tools."

Getting his tools requires going out to his car, checking his phone, realizing he has to return a phone call for another job on the mountain. He then informs you he has to drive to the top of the mountain for a phone signal to get the address, telling you he will be right back.

On a side note, if you are calling a repairman and you've purchased one of the pre-"Staying Alive" (Prior to 1980) houses on the mountain, remember this, nothing will be cheap or easy. The only thing cheap and easy on this mountain is the delivery of firewood because they stop at the farthest spot on your driveway and dump the whole load, effectively blocking your exit until you've stacked it. (A good strategy if you ask me because I have children to go out and do the work.)

The term Mountain Time also applies to any type of meal on the mountain. You cannot go into any place and "grab a quick bite." This is because Lenny, the cook is busy chatting with Beverly the waitress, sidetracked when Dawn, the girl he's been trying to date comes into the restaurant. I remember my first couple of times on the mountain I sat waiting for my breakfast saying, "Gosh, is he grinding the wheat into flour back there for my biscuit?"

Dinner is supposed to be a relaxing casual affair. What I mean by relaxing and casual is plan on quality bonding time waiting for your meal. Many restaurants, staffed for the season have a hard time working any surge of people at any given time. Best bet? Sit back and relax, have another drink. Write your experience up as quality mountain time. After all, you are on vacation, what's the rush?

I think living on Mountain Time has made Beech Mountain some type of time vortex. The locals, or permanent residents don't seem to age up here. That same cashier from 6 years ago, who was already past retirement age, shows up working another job because she, "just likes staying busy." She doesn't look her age because slowing down, like everyone working on the mountain, preserves your body keeping you young. Some say they slow down in the winter to preserve warmth, others in the summer because of the heat (it's 68 degrees for goodness sake) I think they found the fountain of youth.

I remember throwing a Rumplestiltskin at a restaurant because it took 45 minutes getting a meal and the food was wrong. My local friends looked at me saying, "What's your problem? Slow down, you're on Mountain Time."

9. THERE ARE PETS, THEN THERE ARE PETS

Beech Mountain is full of furry friends, some two legged, others four legged. There is no leash law for dogs on the mountain, or cats for that matter. I always tell people visiting, if you do not want to lose your pet, or think there is a possibility of it antagonizing anything then put it on a leash. Why do I tell people this? Because as a runner on the mountain, I've pulled a few Carl Lewis moments getting away from a wayward dog. The cats usually hiss at me in a "Screw Off" kind of way, going about their business. The dogs are much shiftier on this mountain. There is one dog hiding behind a bush most of the mornings I run, I swear she probably has a calendar in the house marking days where "prey is available." I'd run past the house as quietly as possible thinking I could get past her when she'd jump out of the bush going after me. Luckily, she is overweight, and I am in pretty decent shape, and the house is on a downhill so I manage to outrun her.

Another visitor to the mountain, brought his dog, letting him out unleashed to pee before going to bed. The dog, spying a deer in the backyard was gone before anyone could say, "SIT!" Luckily, four hours later, the dog shows up at a house 5 miles away, scratching the door. The occupant, thinking it was an animal not of the canine variety, grabbed his Bowie knife and slowly opened the door. In fell an exhausted, scratched up dog who promptly fell asleep in front of his fireplace. He was tagged, owner and pet were happily reunited. So visiting or living, a leash is a good idea if you have a wanderer.

Beech Mountain has many different hiking trails for animals, but the Emerald Mountain Outback is not one of them. The trails are for mountain bikes and hikers. Throw in an animal and you have something dragging an owner where they don't belong, or something or someone cutting off a mountain biker. That is why the Town of Beech Mountain created the Beech Mountain Bark Park located at the top of the mountain, across from Town Hall in the Meadows. There are two sections dependent on dog size, available water, toys and of course the poopie bags. My rule of thumb with the dog park is to park my little bundle of fur next to the fence gauging the attention of the other dogs making sure everyone looks happy before releasing him/her to the hounds. The good part of the Bark Park is that I've met many new friends as we sit on the benches watching the pooches play.

Animals are allowed at restaurants as long as they have outside seating. This gives you a great place to grab a bite to eat while Fido relaxes under your chair. I use these places for socializing my rescue dog, Shawnee. At any outdoor concert on the mountain you will find many pets and again a leash is a good idea. During the summer Beech Mountain hosts a Dog Derby at Buckeye Recreation Center, where residents compete in contests for Best Trick, Shaggiest Dog, Owner Look A Like (we won that once because my dog looks like Benji and my son refused to cut his blonde hair that summer) Behaved animals are always welcome. One got thrown out of a summer concert for being a horny guy with the ladies.

Once you have established residence, you'll end up with a few unwanted pets. Many people love feeding the birds off of their back porches, and the birds kind of love it to. So do the squirrels, the raccoons and even the errant bear. If you put bird feeders out, it is a good idea to take them in at night and eliminate Yogi from appearing on your porch. I came out one night and Yogi was hanging in the middle of my deck emptying my bird feeder in his mouth. Of course, he looked at me with a, "What? You left out the snack!"

The deer are almost pets on Beech Mountain, and many people leave deer corn for their guests. The deer on this mountain are smart, they seem to realize there is a no hunting on Beech Mountain and periodically graze at the "Entering Beech Mountain" signs silently giving hunters the finger. They also embody the "deer in the headlight" looks for people, dogs, and cars. Remember they will look at you frozen, playing some type of game of chicken until someone decides on fleeing. Your rule of thumb on the mountain is if you feed them, they will come, and they will bring their friends. This applies to people too.

Many people ask me if I worry about the Bears of Beech Mountain. With all the tourists leaving their trash out in trash bins, don't worry, there is always an available food source, meaning not you. If you are looking for bear sighting, your best bet is your local dumpster, or if your neighbors put trash out in their trash cans, get up early and watch the bears raid them. Beech Mountain put together a campaign to put wooden lids on the trash bins. The bears simply laughed, pulling the wood from the side of the bin and pulling the trash cans out from there. If you want to attract bears, leave your trash outside. If you do not want to attract bears, then do the right thing and leave your trash out the morning of pickup omitting the opportunity for a dinner date with Yogi. Or, so what I do, take your trash to the dump at the top of Beech Mountain. There's word around the bear population this is the "All You Can Eat Buffet" place.

There are many other animals on Beech Mountain, usually the ones at night are the ones to look out for - coyotes, bobcats, and of course the tourist who has lost his way. Always remember to steer clear of the skunk. My 3 year old once was running towards one yelling, "Come here kitty."

Luckily I pulled the Olympic runner tackling him before we got sprayed. If you or your pets, including children, ever get sprayed by a skunk, the best way to remove the stink is equal parts of Dawn dishwashing detergent, baking soda and Hydrogen Peroxide. I've also purchased Nature's Miracle, found in most pet stores as my go to item in a clutch. This works with skunk spray, animal musks, dog pee and of course the sick child puking.

There are pets you invite into your life, then there are the ones that come as a surprise. One resident watched a German Shepherd live in the woods behind his house for one brutally cold winter. He fed the dog, which was skittish hiding from everyone, until after 3 months he left the back door open. The dog walked in and sat in front of the fire. He's been a very beloved pet ever since. So if you are not planning on adding any type of animal - raccoon, deer, dog, bear to your menagerie, watch what you feed them and put your trash at the dump.

10. DUMPSTER DIVING

We've already had the discussion about the bear parties in the trash bins outside of homes on Beech Mountain. I had a bin battle with the crows, raccoons and bears deciding it was much easier taking my trash to the dump than cleaning up moldy coffee grounds. The final straw was when the bear decided on blocking my road by pulling my trash bin into the middle of it before emptying the containers onto the street.

The dump sits at the top of Beech Mountain, across from Fred's General Mercantile. The site also includes a recycling area, for those into limiting your footprint on the Earth. It is self sorting, so we keep a large recycling bin in our home, then take the whole thing over to the recycle center, sorting it there. My children are not happy doing this as their hands get sticky and God forbid, sometimes old beer spills on them!

I've passed my thrifty lifestyle down to my children, specifically my youngest who loves dumpster diving! Beech Mountain has some of the best dumpster diving. My youngest took the trash to the dump, and came back with a complete set of outdoor furniture in perfect condition. Glass topped table with four chairs! He was proud of himself when we looked it up online and it was valued over 500 dollars. He's also found artwork, a computer screen, keyboard, and lots of skis and boots. The best times for dumpster diving, according to him are spring and fall. That's when all the part time residents open up or close up their homes for the season. Most homes up here have a mountain decor, so when they decide to get rid of something it usually fits right into our cabin.

The saying is true that one man's trash is another man's treasure. What others throw away, is still perfectly usable to us making it a win/win situation. This is why, if you are looking to decorate your home, the consignment shops of the High Country are valuable resources. The stuff in there is above what they throw away in the dumpster, and usually very good quality at an amazing price. Banner Elk Consignments is one of my favorites, I've found an antique dresser for under $200, and cabin style pictures for a song!

We still regularly take our trash to the dump, and each time a new adventure as the kids dumpster dive. I was waiting while they were picking through the trash and a very nice old lady came up to me. "I have food that I was going to throw away because we are leaving for the season. Do you want it?" Many would be offended at the offer of food, not me. I was given three grocery bags of pasta, orange juice, hot dogs, buns, lunch meat, bread, a few beers and all the condiments I could every want, everything pretty much unopened. The only thing I tossed back into the dumpster was the open jar of peanut butter. I figure I should share the love with the local bears giving back to the community some of my free food. If you are hungry, just hang out by the dump and look a little sad, someone will probably offer you a nice mountain buffet.

****Side note on the Dump:

Today I went over with my recycling, a few trash bags and extra time to chew the fat with the employees.

I arrive as there is excitement at the dump.

Someone has found an old briefcase!

We all look at the corner of the briefcase peeking out from under a bunch of trash in one of the dumpsters.

"What do you think? Should we go for it?" Someone asks.

"Of course, what if there is something in it?" I say, "Look it has an old Eastern Airlines baggage tag on the handle, that really dates it. What if someone took it off an airplane, threw it in their basement for years, then finally took it here without looking in it!"

"Could have money in it," Someone says.

"From Duggie Howser," Someone adds.

"That's the doctor kid on TV Doogie Howser, the dance or are you talking about D.B. Cooper?" I ask.

"Howser, Cooper they sound alike," He says.

"Maybe there is a treasure map inside," Someone else says.

"Or stocks and bonds," another adds.

"We're splitting it, right? Not finders keepers?" I ask thinking of all the books I'd buy with my part of the "treasure."

"Of course," he says, I'm waiting for him to add, "We's all family on the mountain."

We fish the briefcase out, everyone excited because it is LOCKED! Surely that means there is SOMETHING in it! I haven't had this much excitement at the dump since finding my outdoor furniture there!

"Sometimes things are locked for a reason," Someone says as excitement builds.

We all stand around while one person gets a screw driver, forcing open the lock.

"Wow, remind me not to buy this kind of briefcase, I'd be robbed in no time," I say.

"Here goes nothing," he says opening the briefcase.

Damn!

It is empty!

"Oh well, at least it gives me a story," I say as he throws the briefcase back in the dumpster.

Don't worry, there's still treasure waiting in our tiny dump, you just have to look for it!

Like the hand carved 50 lb. wooden Mexican sombrero.

One man's treasure can be another man's treasure!

11. FALL AND FESTIVALS

The High Country of North Carolina comes alive during the fall season. It starts when the first tree turns, prompting everyone from the low country to jump in their cars for what we call "leaf peeping" time. Traffic increases and slows to a standstill on the Blue Ridge Parkway, which I totally understand because some of the views with the colors of fall are completely breath taking! Fall is also a time where the mountains come alive with festivals celebrating everything from apples to the Wizard of Oz.

On Beech Mountain we celebrate fall with an Autumn at Oz festival in September. The 1970's Oz Theme Park, tucked on top of the mountain, comes alive for two days. The park is packed with actors portraying the characters from the movie from Dorothy to Glenda to the Cowardly Lion. Tickets are sold online, proceeds going back into rebuilding this magical place. If you decide to "go off to see the wizard" a few pointers:

1. Tickets go on sale early and sell out very quickly. If you want a particular time watch the LandofOz.com website as popular times usually disappear the first few days. Like the Autumn at Oz Facebook Page and mark your calendar with an alarm, so you are on time purchasing your tickets before they sell out.

2. The Autumn at Oz event coincides with fall, making the park a beautiful place. You are on Beech Mountain, where, as locals say, "If you don't like the weather, wait

15 minutes." The organizers of the festival moved the event from October to September because we had a few weekends were people were walking a yellow brick road covered in snow. September doesn't mean you don't need to plan for all types of weather. There is no rain date for the festival. Plan ahead with the layering (see Do These Boots Make My Butt Look Big) and check local weather prior to attending the park. Everyone loves dressing up like the characters, especially small children.

3. If you own a home on the mountain and come up in the summertime, Beech Mountain Club offers a private Land of Oz tour. Pack a lunch, catch a ride up to the top of the mountain with other club members and recreate the movie as you travel through the theme park. Visit the Beech Mountain Club website www.beechmountainclub.org for dates, usually sometime in July.

4. If you can't make the Autumn at Oz festival, Beech Mountain now promotes June Family Fun Month, opening the Oz park on Fridays during the month of June along with family activities scheduled for every day in June including lodging discounts. There is nothing like escaping the heat, vacationing in cool mountain breezes and visiting the Land of Oz. Information for the Family Fun Month is available on several Beech Mountain websites: LandofOz.com, Town of Beech Mountain, Beech Mountain Chamber of Commerce, and Beech Mountain Resort.

Other Fall Festivals:

OCTOBER - **Wooly Worm Festival** is a fall tradition of the High Country, not located on Beech Mountain but in Banner Elk, just down the mountain. A 40 year + tradition runs the 3rd weekend in October, pitting Wooly Worms or Wooly Bear Caterpillars against each other in heats throughout Saturday and Sunday, the winner not only earning cold hard cash but predicting the winter weather of the High Country for that current season. The winner's brown and black bands are counted for the weeks of winter vs. warmer weather. Worms can be purchased at the festival or brought from your neck of the woods, some training their worms prior to race and creating full habitats for the worm's relaxation.

Valle Country Fair is another tradition off Beech Mountain in Valle Crucis. Some call this an overgrown church bazar located in one of the prettiest fall places, Valle Crucis or Valley of the Cross. This Fair is full of High Country food, from fresh pressed apple cider to homemade apple butter, mountain music, fine art and crafts to family fun and activities.

Note: Both the Wooly Worm and Valle Country Fair occur the same weekend as Appalachian State University's Homecoming Football Game. Some residents of Beech Mountain choose this weekend to hole up in their home, purchasing groceries and wine ahead of time as traffic through Boone and Banner Elk can be quite interesting. Others brave coming off the mountain for some good family fun at these festivals.

JUNE - **A Cool 5 Festival** - Runners and non runners love this weekend of fitness on Beech Mountain in June. A Cool 5 started as a local 5 mile race billed as cool because the race is over 5000 feet in elevation. It is not an easy race with a nice hill climb, but the views and the venue make it worth it. The weekend is filled with music, family activities and fun. Visit Buckeye Recreation Center website for more information on this weekend. One year they decided to rename the race "ClimbMAX" that didn't really go over to well, I, for one, am glad it is back to "A Cool 5."

JULY - **Annual Roasting of the Hog** - Beech Mountain Resort is the location for this Fourth of July festival. Tickets include live music, food and fireworks. The hog is roasted by the Fire Department at the top of the mountain and plates of pulled pork are served with all the fixings. They now offer turkey for those who do not eat pork, and a vegetarian option. This is a great place to relax on a cool night catching up with friends you met during wintertime.

AUGUST - **Crafts on the Green** - local artists take over the yard behind Fred's General Mercantile. Usually held the first weekend in August, this is a great time of the year where everyone off the mountain is sweltering in the Dog Days of summer. Get some inspiration, or find something new for your mountain home while enjoying music, food, art and storytellers.

AUGUST - **Mile High Kite Festival** occurs over Labor Day Weekend. The meadows of Beech Mountain come alive as everyone comes out, trying their hand at flying a kite. The Town of Beech Mountain sells kite kits for flying, music, kite demonstrations including kite fights. One year we had a steady 15/mph breeze all day, several thousand children and adults flying kites. Needless to say getting the kite up in the sky wasn't as hard as trying not to mow down some poor unsuspecting child while keeping it aloft.

DECEMBER - Beech Mountain comes alive with family activities all during the month from a Yule Log to Hayrides for Christmas Trees at Fred's General Mercantile's Christmas Tree Farm to Breakfast with Santa. Check out Buckeye Recreation Center's website for dates and times for all these great activities.

Or, do what I do. Light a fire outside in the summertime, inside in the winter time and curl up with a good book.

A festival of the mind.

12. HOW TO SURVIVE A SNOW VACATION OR, HONEY, WHERE ARE THE KIDS?

Most vacations take some sort of planning and a snow trip to Beech Mountain is not exempt. A little bit of planning before visiting Beech Mountain during the snow season makes an enjoyable vacation. This includes those of us living up here, anxiously awaiting visitors.

If you are flying and renting a vehicle, make sure it covers two basics, all-wheel drive with good tires and plenty of room for snow equipment. The extra cost of the SUV will come in handy when plowing through snow to your cabin, or transporting the family and their gear to the Resort. Some car rentals also include ski racks with their vehicles. Check with your rental agency.

If you are spending all of winter break (usually the last two weeks of December) at the resort, think about purchasing a season pass. You only need to ski the mountain 6 times to break even, many friends purchase the pass, adding extra winter vacations and loving it. The passes go on sale the beginning of October, there is a limited number at a discounted price, make sure you keep an eye out and get yours before they sell out. I purchased my pass and enjoyed over 70 days on the snow. I think I got my money's worth. The season pass sale is announced on all resort social media sites and their website www.beechmountainresort.com

Planning ahead on gear makes that first day on the snow a breeze. If anyone in your group is renting equipment, the best thing to do is get everything the night before you go to the resort. This cuts out sweating in lines in snow gear, getting boots fit while sweating in snow gear and paying for things while sweating in snow gear. I cannot tell you how many families I watch, sweating, looking like they sucked on a tree full of lemons waiting in rental lines. Many visitors to this mountain come in groups, meaning that rentals are included in the group price, it may be your luck that you show up at rentals just as a Coach bus lets out 100 people ahead of you. As you drive up the mountain consider the several ski shops along the way wanting to help, including the Resort renting the night before. Take advantage and rent your equipment early.

Gear check. Prior to driving to the mountain, sit down every member of your group and do a dry run on their equipment. Remember when I said, "There is no such thing as being cold, only inappropriate clothing?" Forgetting something can be trivial or it can ruin your day.

The basic checklist:
Long Underwear or some type of base layer
Good socks - not your basic cotton socks, but specific wool snow socks
Fleece or hoodie.
Snow pants
Snow jacket
Helmet
Googles
Face mask or neck warmer
Dry, warm waterproof gloves
Hand warmers
Lip Balm
Lift Ticket or Season Pass

I hit all the summer sales and thrift stores in the mountains, amassing a collection of socks, gloves, face masks, hats and goggles. Probably because with boys, things disappear on a regular basis. I can't stress enough the importance of socks and gloves. Many a day is ruined because fingers or toes get wet and cold.

Helmet you ask? Remember, at the resort most of our visitors are from Florida. There is no snow in Florida, so many are seeing snow for the first time. I always tell my children while strapping a helmet on them, "I'm not worried about what you are doing, I'm scared to death of the person flying like a bullet down the slope behind you." I always tell them the helmet is protecting their greatest asset, and I'm not talking about their bum.

Think about lessons. Many are now saying, "How hard can it be? I don't need a lesson." Lessons are beneficial in two ways. If you are a good skier skiing with a beginner friend, it gives you an hour break before you are stuck back on the bunny slope with your friend. And If they get hurt isn't it better if it is not on your watch? Also, lessons start with the most important part of being on the snow, how to get up. Learning how to do it properly the first time, saves lots of time and frustration later. Beech Mountain offers group and individual lessons, I've always gone the route of an individual lesson for the one on one time. Sometimes if the lift lines look really crowded, I've purchased a lesson to jump the lift line AND learn a few new skills in the process.

What about my kids? The best deal on Beech Mountain for children is First Traxx (5 and up) and Snow Kamp. An all day camp, children are grouped together by ability, then alternate between playing inside and instruction outside on the snow. The Resort's concept is safety, fun and instruction. Rentals, lift tickets, and lunch is included in the per person price. Not only does this give you a break from 830a to 330p to enjoy the snow, camp lets out an hour and a half prior to day session ending, giving the children time to show you newly acquired skills. Remember everyone is looking for a fun vacation, so these camps fill fairly quickly. You can register online for the camp, or show up 830a the day of for registration. The fee you pay is non refundable, so it is best to check the weather prior to registering. One of my favorite sites is Ray's Weather www.averyweather.com for next day's information.

Babies? There is an onsite nursery for a fee.

Snow tubing is back on Beech Mountain. After being gone for a few years, snow tubing is back on the mountain. Did you know that snow tubing started as far back as the 1820's in the Alpine Mountains? Riders speed down a hill on an inflated tube or "doughnut," a slight incline at the bottom stopping their speed. Think of tubing like sledding but in a controlled environment with an inflated tube. Barriers along the sides of the lanes prevent tubers from running into each other on or off of the course. A magic carpet takes riders and tubes back to the top for another run. I always tell visitors if they are unsure they can handle a full day on the snow, snow tubing is a great alternative. Purchase tickets for a scheduled time, ride down the tubing runs as much as you can in your allotted hour. Many enjoy doing this besides skiing or snowboard because the biggest skill it requires is keeping your butt inside the tube, and putting your feet down to stop.

Ice Skating is also available. The earliest ice skating happened in Finland over 3,000 years ago, luckily we are not using that equipment. A frozen rink in the middle of Beech Mountain Resort's Alpine Village is available for ice skaters. Skate rentals are available, as well as walkers for those needing a little help standing up. If you are around after session during the week, you may hear rumblings of a pick up ice hockey game.

Are the only snow sports on the mountain at Beech Mountain Resort? No!

The Town of Beech Mountain has a free sledding hill for children 14 years old and younger. Rental equipment is not provided, bring your own equipment and have some fun. Standing at the bottom and looking up at the hill, the left side is for younger children, the right for older children, meaning the right is steeper and tends to be used more. Watch for a few minutes, gauging out the territory. You'll scope out the places to avoid and have fun watching everyone else bust it! There's always the super Dad, putting the small child in the sled in front of him and hurling down the older kid hill. Every time I watch a family play on the hill, there's always a dip towards the bottom that sends everyone flying from the sled. Most get up walking away with a bruise or two, along with a lesson learned.

Buckeye Recreation Center offers snow shoeing hikes. This is a great way to see our winter wonderland on foot without the skis or snowboard. Several trails take you through the woods, by creeks and out to beautiful views. Visit www.buckeyerec.org for more details and dates for the hikes.

Of course with over 85 inches of snow a season, you can always simply stay home and build your own snowman or igloo. I've driven past several snowball fights in someone's back yard on my way to the resort!

The big thing to remember on a snow vacation is preparation. This includes planning for food, planning for warmth, and planning activities. A little bit of planning goes a long way!

13. NO SNOW? NO PROBLEM!

Many friends are shocked when I tell them I ski in North Carolina. Beech Mountain, located 5506 feet above sea level gets its own share of natural snow, but resorts need to make money, and trusting Mother Nature is a sure way of losing money. Beech Mountain Resort, like most Southern snow resorts adds to its natural snowfall with the help of snowmakers, snow guns, or snow cannons, machines that supplement the natural snow by blowing man-made snow. Invented in 1950 by Art Hunt, Dave Richey, Wayne Pierce, The Grossingers Catskill Resort Hotel in New York became the first in the world using man-made snow.

What's the difference between natural and man-made snow? Natural snow tends to be fluffy, or what some of us ski bums call powder. The classic natural snowflake is six sided when it falls from the sky. It is fluffy at first because it is made of air, but as it hits the ground and melts, different ends break off. Or as we play through it, we break off parts of that snowflake. Snowmakers make a different kind of snow.

How does snowmaking work? It is pretty simple. Snowmaking begins at a lake or reservoir. On Beech Mountain, you can find the lake at the bottom of the resort. Water is pumped through large pipes up the mountain through intricate pipe systems to trails in need of snow. The compressors Beech Mountain uses are in a large building in the buildings below Parking Lot 1. When the resort first opened old navy ship compressors pumped water to the snow makers on the mountain. Many of the newer snow makers have a compressor built into the machine, all that is needed is water and electricity. At this point a nucleating agent is added to the water. Talk English you say? This agent allows the most amount of water to freeze into ice crystals or snow. Beech Mountain Resort uses SnowMax.

Here I get a little techy. You are welcome to skip the next paragraph or two and continue on, or, if you have the same curiosity, then read on.

SnowMax Snow Inducer, created in 1987 is a product that enhances snowmaking. In a nutshell, it is a protein derived from the bacteria Pseudomonas syringae. What does this unpronounceable bacteria do? It bonds to the water, making it freeze quicker. A droplet of water is in constant motion, and it must slow down enough forming a hexagonal array for freezing. The goal of a snow guns output is having the most amount of water hitting the ground in the form of snow, SnowMax makes this possible by freezing droplets of water quicker than nature could, making the maximum amount of snow. A bacteria you ask? Yes, this is a naturally occurring bacteria in nature, biodegradable and harmless to animals, plants and the uncontrolled skier. SnowMax comes in a pellet form, which is mixed with the water pumped to the snow guns on the resort. I've heard many a Beech Mountain Resort employee gleefully say, "There's nothing like the smell of SnowMax in the morning!"

Which brings me to the reservoirs and the snow they produce. I can't tell you how many parents I've watched let their children eat the snow, simply because it is so white and beautiful. That beautiful white snow starts down in the reservoir as green colored water eventually coming out as the fluffy white stuff kids stick in their mouths. When my children attempted eating snow, I took them down to the lake, showing them the water, solving that problem immediately. I won't mention the people spitting on the snow, throwing things they shouldn't throw etc. Of course everyone knows why you shouldn't eat yellow snow, this is why you shouldn't eat man made snow.

Back to snowmaking, it takes more than water, SnowMax, and pumps. It also takes what we call "The Snow Gods." There are a lot of variables going into making snow, the first factor is the ambient temperature, meaning it must be cold outside to make snow. Heck, it must be cold outside for it to snow naturally. Snow can be made at 32 degrees F, but this snow could be slushy. The optimum temperature for snowmaking is 28 degrees or less. The second factor is humidity or your "wet bulb" temperature. Simply put, too much humidity in the air does not allow water to evaporate and water needs to evaporate in order to cool down or freeze. That is why sometimes the temperature could be at or below freezing but it is raining because the humidity does not allow the cooling of water to a frozen state. An ideal snowmaking condition is a temperature of 30 degrees F and a humidity in the 30% range. Once the temperature falls below 20 degrees F into the teens, the humidity is not as much a factor.

The third factor is getting the maximum amount of snow on the ground. Beech Mountain Resort's newer snowmakers with their specialized nozzles blow a larger surface area, covering more with snow. Some of the older equipment, not as specialized as the stationary snow blowers, supplement in areas in need of extra snow.

Finally the fourth factor is Super cooling. There are two types of snowmakers: *air water guns* and *fan guns*. Air water guns are mounted guns that combine water and cold air to make snow. Fan guns, or airless guns, look like jet engines—the air is provided by a small nozzle surrounded by a fan, and the water is fed through rings of nozzles into the fan airstream and cooled. Sometimes you will see employees of Beech Mountain Resort walking down the slope in black jumpsuits tending to the blowers. They knock all the ice off of the water pipes to the blowers, making sure they don't freeze, reposition the blowers to make sure snow is blowing in the right direction, then they hold their arm in front of the spray. They are looking at the output of the blower, ensuring it is in a frozen state and not water, due to many of the above factors. These people work long hours, deep into the night, in the harshest conditions, usually getting pretty wet making sure the best product possible is ready for those of us craving 9am "first tracks."

Mid-November, residents of Beech Mountain tune their ears in the direction of the resort, waiting patiently. There's nothing more exciting than hearing the first hum of the season as the resort turns on the snowmakers. Computers now take over the nuances of temperature, humidity, etc., taking it down to an exact science, making sure when the guns are on, the maximum amount of output is achieved.

Once the snow is on the ground, the job moves over to the groomers. Beech Mountain Resort proudly uses Pisten Bully Machines or Groomers, move the snow mother nature or snow makers produces onto the trails. How does a Groomer work? There is talent and science in the seats of those large machines. Preparing the slopes starts as the season ends for the year. Once the snowpack from the season melts and dries, crews check the trails for downed trees and stumps cutting these away. Mowing on the slopes is usually done twice in the off season, though on Beech Mountain the trails that are part of the Downhill Biking System are mowed more frequently.

The first snow of the season is when machines are prepared but not running just yet. The start of grooming depends on the amount of snow mother nature or snow machines provide. The goal is to get a specific base bonding with the frozen ground before grooming. Once the base layer is created and the top layers either blown by guns or dumped by Mother Nature, the big Pisten Bullies go to work. A

Groomer is a diesel powered machine with a front mounted hydraulic blade for pushing snow and a tiller for shaping snow. The result from the roller is what snow enthusiasts call "Corduroy." These machines travel up and down the slopes preparing them for the day ahead. They can handle the grade of the slopes due to a low center of gravity and large contact area. They warn skiers and snowboarders when they are in the area with a loud beeping. Groomers looks for a minimum of 2-3 inches of base as anything smaller means "flipping" the base, pulling up that bottom layer that could include rocks and grass. No one wants to see anything but white on a ski slope, right?

Smaller Park Pisten Bully Machines run through the Terrain Park of the resort, while other employees hand rake ramps and jumps of the park. This work is done middle of the night to early morning. If you are living or staying close to the resort, take a peak out your window around 6am and you may spy a Groomer running down White Lightening. When you see the snowmaking team and the groomers out on the slopes, remember to thank them. Without them you wouldn't have such a beautiful and fun place to play!

14. CAN I GIVE YOU A LIFT?

Beech Mountain Resort has 17 runs from easy Beginner to a Black Diamond, depending upon your skill level. There are a total of 8 lifts, one high speed quad, one fixed grip quad, 4 doubles, one Magic Carpet and a rope tow.

High Speed Quad - also called a Detachable Quad or Express Quad. This is the fastest lift on the resort. Chairs run on a wire cable suspended between towers. Detached chairs run faster than their Fixed Grip counterparts, also giving employees the chance to remove chairs during extreme or severe weather, reducing stress on the cable and the towers. The High Speed Quad is located at the base of the resort in the Alpine Village. This lift takes you to the summit of the resort, the runs from the top Blue (intermediate) and black (expert), and to 5506, the SkyBar. It also provides access over a bridge to the backside of the mountain to Oz Run (intermediate).

Your runs from the High Speed Quad are:

> **ShawneeHaw** - Intermediate run from the summit to either a beginner run through Play Yard or an intermediate in Powder Bowl. When open, the Meadows is also part of the Terrain Park system of the resort. (See Terrain Park Etiquette) ShawneeHaw is the Cherokee name for a tree, the Serviceberry blooming in spring.

Robbins Run - An Intermediate run to mid mountain, continuing onto Beginner Run ShawneeHaw to Play Yard. This run was named after Grover Robbins, the man behind Tweetsie Railroad, a local Wild West attraction of the High Country and Land of Oz, an amusement park on top of Beech Mountain. The Oz park ran for several years before closing in 1981. There are still parts of Oz remaining tucked back behind the resort on top of the mountain. Private tours are available as well as the Autumn At Oz festival in October and Family Fridays during the month of June. (See Festivals)

Southern Star - Black Diamond to mid mountain, connecting with Beginner Run ShawneeHaw and Play Yard.

White Lightening - Black Diamond to the bottom of the mountain, connecting with lower Play Yard. White Lightening was originally called High Dive due to the lip between the top of the run which is Intermediate, to the face, the steepest part of Beech Mountain Resort.

Fixed Grip Doubles - The chairs are fixed, they cannot be removed from the rope. Doubles mean two people maximum to a chair. These lifts are slower than the High Speed Quad Lift running approximately 5MPH compared to the 12MPH of the High Speed. Lift 6 starts by the Lodge and Ski School, running to the summit of the mountain, (See above runs).

Lifts 3 and 4 are also double chairs servicing the easiest (green) runs of the mountain. They run from just above the loading point of the High Speed Quad to mid Mountain. These are beginner lifts, running at a slow speed. They service the Play Yard, a Beginner trail of the mountain.

Lift 1, a double chair runs from the bottom of Play Yard to the top of Lower ShawneeHaw. This run is a beginner (green) run, a great step up from Lifts 3 and 4 in length and skill level.

Oz Lift - a fixed grip quad (4 person) lift runs from the bottom of Oz Run on the backside of the mountain to the summit. The Oz Run is Intermediate, a great alternative when the two Intermediate runs, Shawnee Haw and Robbins Run become crowded. A word of warning on Oz, if it is a windy day, check the run before venturing down. The run points west past the theme park and a stiff, windy day can make it extremely cold and hard travel. If the lift is empty and not many are venturing over the bridge to the run, think twice. Or do what I do and go anyway, cursing yourself as the wind pushes you back up the run, and the lift ride to the top is freezing.

Finally, **The Magic Carpet**, beginner in the School Yard, is the best people watching place at the resort. The School Yard is where Ski School starts lessons, using the Magic Carpet to take new users from the bottom of the School Yard to the top. It is a moving carpet you step on, taking you to the top where you casually step off. Easier said than done for newbies. I've enjoyed a beer outside at the picnic tables of the Lodge watching new snow enthusiasts navigating the Magic Carpet. It is funnier than the Three Stooges (if you don't know who the Three Stooges are, look it up. You'll be glad you did). Even better was the old J Bar lift of the School Yard, requiring users to grab a bar which pulled them on the snow. It's removal and the installation of the Magic Carpet were very nice additions to the learning process.

You can always start at the resort maps, determining your first lift ride of the day based on your skill level. Don't join the Mile High Club (see Mile High Club) stay within your limits and enjoy your day on the snow!

15. SLOPES ARE OPENING, KNOW THE LINGO

Sometimes people are talking to you in English, but you cannot understand a word they are saying. Just like skiers and snowboarders on the slopes, there's a lingo specific to Beech Mountain ski slopes many may not understand. I thought I would help you with a few terms:

Jerry - An individual who lacks true understanding of the sport or life in general. Some even call them "dumbasses" on the slope.

Bullet - the novice skier who does not understand how to turn in order to slow down. Therefore they shoot right past you like a bullet until wiping out at the bottom of the slope.

ID 10 T - look at it closely, see if you get it. These people stand in the lift line holding their skis, getting offended when told, "You have to put your skis on to ride the lift."

Accidental Chairers - those not realizing once your chair reaches the top of the lift, you must exit the chair. They tend to continue riding around the dismount area until crashing off the chair, or a liftie has to stop the lift helping them off.

Purposeful Chairers - Those that reach the top of the slope and decide the only thing they want to do is ride the chair BACK down. Again, you'll see them continuing on the chair past the dismount section.

Hedge Hog - That person exiting the slope by way of bushes, usually not coming out for quite a while.

Flying Squirrel - that person you see flying down the slopes, their coat unzipped showing off their Florida sweatshirt, poles in hand, out to the side, frozen look of fear on their face until they crash. If you hear someone yell "Squirrel!" jump out of the way. They don't have ADD, there is a Flying Squirrel coming your way.

Miracle - that person, usually after an extended visit to the bar, has the most epic crash you've ever seen. Everyone waits for ski patrol to cart them off the slopes but you watch their hands come up out of the pile in the snow and you hear, "Whooooooo!"

Hibernating Hedge Hog - That person sitting in the trees or bushes waiting for spring to avoid continuing down the ski slope.

Zombie - that person who fell in the snow, slowly pulling himself by his elbows to the side of the slope.

Yard Sale - the perfect wipeout consisting of losing hat, goggles, gloves, poles, skis and periodically, pants.

Rag Doll - the position of the body in the air when a snowboarder hits unexpected dips in the terrain. Usually followed by some type of Yard Sale.

Scorpion - the fall bringing the legs up over the head in the shape of a scorpion stinger. This sometimes also includes some type of Rag Doll.

Rolling Down The Windows - a skier's attempt on a jump quickly realizing it is over their head. As they try to right themselves, they "roll down the windows" or roll their arms usually screaming until they face plant in the snow their skis coming up in a "double scorpion."

Popsicle - that snowboarder/skier coming down the slopes in front of blowing snow guns. Becomes a recognizable person in spring. Also referred as the "Human Popsicle"

Tourist - that person dressed in the sub zero parka, with three layers underneath, hat, gloves, hand warmers and face mask on a Carolina Bluebird 45 degree day.

16. WHAT NOT TO SAY ON THE CHAIRLIFT RIDE

On one of my chairlift rides to the top, a very sweet old man jumped on the chair next to me, as we were riding up, he looked at me with a wicked smile saying, "Is it windy today or are you just blowing me away?"

Ugh.

You may plan on coming to a ski resort and meeting the love of your life, I thought I'd share with you how to scare people on the chairlift.

Stare at the person next to you without saying a word, the entire ride from the bottom to the top.

Ask if the guy next to you has eaten or needs money. The worn out, almost in tatters ski gear look is definitely a local "ain't nobody got time for matching" clothes look. That's usually the tourists.

Offer them a healthy dollop of chewing tobacco on the way to the top. (Some may actually take you up on that)

Tell us you've been to Colorado, Utah, The Swiss Alps, Argentina, or Sugar Mountain. Most locals here have been there too. Oh, and we don't ski only one week a season, we ski all season here THEN go out west for that extra week or so. Let us tell you where we've been to......

Ask them how you get down from the top.

Bang your equipment on my equipment. I'll give you one bang as a "gimme," but if you do it repeatedly, you are not getting my "positive" attention.

Pull the chairlift safety rail down without acknowledging first, usually resulting in banging someone on the head with it. I always wear a helmet, but some do not and will not appreciate it.

Food you should not pull out of your jacket on a Southern Ski Resort:

Pigs Feet

Pickles

Pimento Cheese

Okra

Vienna Sausage

Smoked Salmon - seriously, I was offered this on the chairlift, my breath cost me a few friendships that day.

Do not tell me about your last relationship. I really don't want to know.

Ask me if I recognize you without saying your name. With a helmet, hat, goggles, ski mask, I have no idea who you are. (See Do These Boots Make My Butt Look Big, Old Friends)

Ask people quietly, "Did I see them working on the lift this morning? or, Did anyone see that bolt on the ground?"

Follow it up with, "I hope we get stuck today."

Instead, make each ride to the top bearable with casual conversation. Everyone is used to the "where are you from" conversation starters, a much better choice than any of the above. You will find that you will end up with the same people during the day as everyone skis close to the same speed down, until you decide taking a break takes precedent. Keep your conversation respectful, don't have people purposely trying to avoid riding with you.

17. DON'T JOIN THE MILE HIGH CLUB

I am sure you've heard about the Mile High Club, but I'm not talking about **that** Mile High Club. (The one involving airplanes and bathrooms and a few odds and ends.) I'm talking about two very different Mile High Clubs on Beech Mountain, one you'll want to join and one you will not want to join.

Let's start with a few facts. At 5,506 feet above sea level, the Town of Beech Mountain is the highest incorporated Town East of the Rockies. With a local population of over 300 full time residents, Beech Mountain's population soars to over 10,000 during the winter season and 5,000 during the summer season, not to mention those who pass through during fall. Many of those 10,000 making Beech Mountain their ski vacation, fall victim to the "Mile High Club." This is when everyone in their group, all experienced, take the novice to the lift telling them, "Don't worry, this is a pretty easy mountain, you'll be just fine."

I've watched people standing in the lift line holding their skis, getting upset when the attendant explains to them, "You have to have your equipment on to ride the lift." The reason they get upset is that they don't know how to put the equipment on. I watched one man standing in gravel attempting to put his skis on backwards. These poor unsuspecting souls then ride the lift to the top, where their friends happily say, "See you at the bottom" and ski off. If you've never skied before, and your friends are taking you to the lift that takes you to the top, remember, the only way down in the winter is on the snow. You cannot ride the lift back down, and you cannot hitch a ride on a snowmobile. You'll just have to figure out how to make it back down. One poor woman took 2 1/2 hours alternately skiing then walking, then skiing until she finally collapsed in a heap at the bottom, where her friends were waiting saying, "Are you ready to do it again?"

I've watched poor souls spend a good hour at the top, talking themselves into skiing to the bottom, only to get tangled in the orange webbing on the side of a slope designed to keep people from crashing onto decks or through windows of houses. Others just go to the bar at the top, figuring a little liquid courage would make the ride to the bottom a little easier. It only serves to loosen you up, so when you do crash, and you will, it may not hurt as much. Do what I did when I returned to the slopes after a 10 year hiatus. My friends directed me over to the lift saying, "OK, let's go to the top."

I stopped, refusing to move. "I'll get on that lift when an instructor tells me to." And guess what, I had the most enjoyable day!

"5506" is an umbrella bar located at the top of the Beech Mountain Resort. Umbrella bar means on a beautiful day, some times during the winter, but more often during the summer, the roof retracts like an umbrella letting in that cool mountain breeze. Food and drink are served at the location. Everyone hanging out in that bar during any season of the year are a happy bunch, partially because alcohol consumed at a high altitude affects quickly and the view from the deck of the bar is to die for. You can see forever. I've heard rumblings about the "Mile High Club" of 5506, but haven't asked what it entails. My sweet husband and I used to work for the airlines, we've already joined that one.

A short walk behind the bar up the hill will take you to a cliff where you can see all of the valley of Banner Elk down below, Sugar Mountain in the distance and the profile peaks of Grandfather Mountain. There is a fence separating the Land of Oz from Beech Mountain Resort property. Please recognize this and keep off the Oz Property, you can see the same view from the cliff behind "5506" as you can without the danger of trespassing onto Oz property and getting arrested.

Whatever the season on Beech Mountain, remember, what goes up must come down. In the winter time if you decide to hit the bar, you must have ski equipment and the only way down after that hot toddy is on the snow. Perhaps limit yourself to one hot toddy at the top planning your next one at the bottom. During the summer time you can take the lift up to the "5506" or the Sky Bar, but you must take the lift back down. Keep track of the time when it gets close to the lift closing. Missing your ride means a long walk down a steep slope to your car.

There is a way to drive up to "5506" for your libation, but I'll leave it to the locals to give you directions. That way I'm not blamed for with the crowds parking at the top. You cannot park at the top, that is private property and you will get towed. If you do find your way to the top, park at the Emerald Outback parking and hike up to the bar, working off the calories you plan on adding at the bar.

However you decide to join the Mile High Club, remember drink responsibly, ski or snowboard responsibly and your vacation will be more the merrier as a result.

18. TERRAIN PARK ETIQUETTE or WATCH OUT!

Beech Mountain Resort's The Park is located on the old tubing hill with a rope tow system. A Terrain Park is a system of items for skiers and snowboarders to practice tricks, including several jumps for those intrepid enough. Some of the items located in the park include:
Pipes
Boxes
Rails
Cannons

Some of the lingo includes:
Money Booters - Large jumps, if you are unexperienced stay away from these.
Kickers - smaller jumps, you'll still get hurt
Donkey D*ck - I'm just leaving this here, I'm not even explaining this one.
Shotgun Rail

The park features may look fun to a beginner on the mountain, but, just like hitting the regular slopes, know your limit and stick within it. The best piece of advice in the park is to be respectful. Rules in the park loosely follow rules of a skate park.

If you are preparing to use a feature, wait your turn. If there is a group of people waiting, there will be some semblance of order to "dropping in" or taking your turn. Before you drop in, call out "dropping in" pause making sure no one has already started ahead of you.

If you are watching someone try out a trick, stay clear of all the other features of the park. Stand in a place where other riders cannot accidentally "take you out" if something goes wrong on the feature. If you are new to this, watch some of the other riders, usually there's someone taking pictures or filming showing the best place to stay out of the way.

Once you complete the trick or feature, whether the outcome was worthy of an upload to YouTube, or the crash that epic,

Get out of the way.

The only reason you should be downslope of a jump or feature for any period of time is because you are hurt and cannot move. If this is the case, yell to someone or make sure someone sees you, stopping other traffic from that feature until you can collect all your gear (say you had a **yardsale**, meaning a crash losing your poles, your goggles, your face mask and other non attached items. Hopefully you had on a helmet otherwise include hat with the list) or until ski patrol arrives. Many skiers will hold their poles in an "X" or snowboarders holding their arms in an "X" while someone recovers from a botched feature.

Always remember, if you cannot see above you anywhere in the park or on the slopes, the person on the snow above you cannot see you.

Park employees work hard all day preparing the park for riders. This means if the park has over 30 features, the employees are out there during the day hand grooming the ramps to the features with a park rake. Sometimes you'll see these employees riding the lifts with a large red or silver rakes in hand. If you are enjoying the park, don't forget to thank them.

A big No No: do not do little jumps off the ramps leading to the features or what's called side hitting them. Typically, you'll find a smaller beginner jump for those new to the park, with larger jumps for the more experienced. If you take the side of a ramp leading to a feature, you're ruining that ramp for those using the feature. If you hear yelling after doing this, it is your own fault, don't use the ramps as little side jumps.

Last but not least, stay within your ability. Test your skills with the smaller features, watch the other riders on the larger features. Enjoy the camaraderie in the park, the cheers when someone hits a new trick, and possibly learn some skills while leaving in one piece.

19. OH! THE SCENERY!

There are many mountain traditions based on season, with the usual way of viewing, here's a better way if you decide on adventure.

Fall Foliage - Every hike on Beech Mountain is beautiful in the fall. Remember if you are coming from the lowlands, fall comes early on this mountain. The positive part is you get to experience fall twice! Fall typically starts on this mountain late September/early October. Some of the best vantage points for the fall leaves are on the Emerald Mountain Outback Hiking/Biking trails. 1.5 miles into the loop trail starting at Wizard's Way, look for Pride Rock which gives you an amazing view of the valley. OZ Rock 2 miles into the trail shows you all of Elk River/Roan Mountain. We like to pack a picnic and enjoy an afternoon on either of those rocks during a crisp fall day.

Fourth of July - fireworks are best from the top of a mountain. Hike to either Pride Rock or Oz Rock and you'll see over 15 different fireworks displays from Tennessee to North Carolina. Some of us pack a picnic and hang out at 5506, the Skybar on the resort. Fireworks usually start right after dusk, which at that time of year is well past 9pm.

Cross Country Skiing - there are several flat trails on the mountain, perfect for cross country skiing on a winter day. If you are new to the sport, The High Country Ski Shop located in Pineola, NC offers cross country ski rentals. If you have skis or want adventure off of Beech Mountain, Roan Mountain is the perfect place!

Swimming Holes - two of the mountains most popular trails offer a great place for a quick dip in cool mountain water. Lower Pond Creek has several sliding rocks along with pools for swimming while Buckeye Falls Trail offers a water fall with a pool at the bottom for a quick dip.

Summer time fun - Buckeye Recreation Center offers several programs for summer fun - rent or borrow a mountain bike, borrow a fishing rod or borrow a canoe. Plan a family afternoon at the lake with a picnic that provides fun but doesn't break the bank.

Waterfalls - Beech Mountain has two beautiful waterfall hikes on the mountain. From moderate to strenuous, these hikes always end with a beautiful water view. Best time for waterfall hiking is after a hard rain. It feels like you've stepped off the planet, the water is so forceful.

Buckeye Falls - Buckeye Falls hike is located at Buckeye Recreation Center on the backside of Beech Mountain. The trailhead is just off the track behind the recreation center, framed in a tall wooden trellis. This trail takes you down the side of the mountain to the waterfall at the bottom. A picnic table for lunch, and a cool bridge for sunning make this a favorite spot on the mountain. During late summer, as you hike from the waterfall over to Buckeye Lake, look along the trail for blackberry bushes. The fruit is smaller than what you normally see in the store but very, very sweet. We've collected enough one summer for a blackberry cobbler.

Lower Pond Creek a 1 mile on the strenuous side hike to a beautiful waterfall. Most take this trail for trout fishing, but the waterfall will captivate you. Bring a hammock and enjoy an afternoon of reading, sit on a large rock next to Pond Creek and enjoy watching the water flash through, or take a swim in the pool created by the waterfall at the bottom. If you are thinking about using any of the large rocks as sliding rocks on this hike, remember the wet rocks usually have moss on them as well and can be very slippery. Oh, and the water is VERY cold.

These two waterfalls are the more famous, there are also smaller falls on other trails on the mountain. It is always a nice surprise following a creek and coming upon a waterfall, like Zig Zag falls of Emerald Mountain Outback. Always remember when hiking on Beech Mountain, leave no trace and take only pictures, we want it just as beautiful the next time your feet hit the trail.

20. MOISTURE, OR LACK THERE OF…

On Beech Mountain, there are two extremes when it comes to moisture in the air, too much or too little. I'm not talking about the snow of winter or the rains of every other season, I'm talking about the humidity.

Wintertime Dry Air. Sitting in front of a roaring fire while watching the snow fall outside your window is a comfortable, relaxing scene. What you don't realize is that cold air swirling around outside is pulling out whatever moisture is left in the air. This results in skin resembling salt flats, hair feeling like straw and of course, those nice electrical shocks when you pet the cat. Not to mention how happy your sinuses are without any moisture,the result, congestion. Your sinuses need gooey mucus (I know, disgusting) to effectively keep viruses and other bad guys from making you sick. Not to mention dry nostrils are more likely to crack and cause nosebleeds.

How does this happen? First of all, the cold air coming into your home has very little moisture, the chill causing you to start a fire or crank up the heat, the warm air pulling more moisture from the air. What little moisture you had on your body quickly evaporates into the air.

The first place on your body you'll notice dry skin is your lips. During the wintertime, I always carry some type of lip moisture. I get so obsessed with lip moisture that we have a bin sitting in the house holding all the open tins of Rose Salve, Chapstick, Carmex and other brands. My husband calls this the lip staging area, moving everything from the pockets in the laundry room to an easy accessible area available to anyone leaving the house. Rose Salve has always been my favorite lip moisture, it also works wonders on chaffed cheeks from the wind and blowing snow.

Next on your agenda all winter long is rehydration. This means drinking water, lots and lots of water to combat the dry air. Many friends mention they drink a lot of beer at apres ski but alcohol tends to dehydrate rather than hydrate. Sure enjoy your apres ski, but my rule of thumb is matching each beer with glass of water, or just water all day long. If you don't like the taste of water, think about adding fruit pieces to it, or tea, making it more palatable.

Home Humidifiers are a great way of adding moisture to your home. If you cannot afford a whole home humidifier, at least purchase a room humidifier for use when you are sleeping at night. You will be shocked at how well you sleep. Remember, keep these appliances super clean as mold and other critters could wreak havoc.

Think twice about that long, hot shower. Long, hot showers feel fantastic after freezing for a day on the slopes, but the longer your body stays in the hot water the more moisture it pulls from your skin. Another good rule of thumb is to limit showers or baths in the wintertime to under 15 minutes or until you are clean. Warm water is better than hot, and 5 minutes usually works. Use a gentle soap that does not strip the natural oils from your skin.

Finally, a good moisturizer goes a long way. Another staple in my pocket is some type of hand moisturizer, along with another in my car. After your bath or shower, pat your skin dry, don't rub the towel over it like you are exfoliating, you'll take away what moisture you have left. Follow up with a good moisturizer (oil based works well) on the damp skin, sealing in moisture and hydrating.

With a little bit of moisturizer and a whole lot of water, you can make your winter visit much more pleasurable!

Which brings me to summer, where the scales tip the other way.

Humidity, definition please:
(h)yoo͞ˈmidədē/
noun
noun: **humidity**
1   the state or quality of being humid.
- a quantity representing the amount of water vapor in the atmosphere or a gas.

That simple phrase means so much on this mountain, for your home, your body and your lifestyle. Since I was talking about rehydrating the body above, let me explain humidity now.

Your body contains over 19 million cells. When the change of seasons moisture arrives, every single cell will soak up the moisture. Soak it up. At the beginning of warm humid weather, I swear my body swells another size until it gets used to the moisture and regulates.

My hair never recovers with the return of moisture, going from the dry plastered straight look to the "Medusa" look of summer. Every wonder why so many women on this mountain have their hair in hats or hair ties during the summer? Because that's the only way of taming it. You can use gels or mousse, calming the frizzles, but luckily everything is so casual on this mountain, you don't need to take the time! I once straightened my curly hair for a dinner date, sporting a fantastic "fro" into the restaurant 20 minutes later! You will feel like you have so much more hair, but it's just the same amount of hair holding on to the extra moisture.

Humidity also means that most of the things in your home will feel damp. They are not specifically damp, they just feel that way. And being a little moist, all of your clothes will wrinkle if you simply breath on them. Every wonder why most of the outdoor clothing is made of wrinkle resistant fabric? Not because we are lazy, but because we can't keep things from wrinkling. This extra moisture can be bad for snow gear. Make sure everything is dried properly and hanging inside your home keeping mold at bay. Better yet, dry properly then seal up in extra large ZipLock bags.

Remember, I mentioned my body swells from the added moisture? So does everything in your house. Windows become difficult to close, drawers simply refuse and you'll find your bedroom doors scraping over wooden floors. What to do?

One possibility is a house dehumidifier, or a room one for the worst part of the home. In my house, the upstairs stays semi dry during the summer, the downstairs not so much. I walked into a bedroom one summer afternoon and almost slipped on the invisible layer of moisture on the wooden floor. If part of your home and garage are underground, you'll have to be vigilant about mold forming on items. Either keep them sparkling clean, or move them to a less moist part of your household. That means clothing, coolers, and anything made of wood, as this really attracts the moisture. Summertime could be a good purging time for your home. Move out what you don't need and is likely to attract mold.

Everyone thinks snow gear is fine sitting in the garage in their home, but be careful. I had a pair of skis fall over during summer. They sat on the moist concrete floor of my garage until the start of snow season. They "pitted" or rust formed around all the of the edges, me thinking they were gone forever. It took Charlie, of Beech Mountain Resort a lot of time and a whole lot of love getting those skis back where they belonged. Now I keep all of our snow gear in a closet built in the garage, so a child cannot knock them over again. You can also take all of your snow gear to a local shop and have them put "summer wax" on your gear, giving you another layer of protection from the moisture of summer.

Sogginess. Extra moisture in the air also affects everything in the kitchen. All your staples should be sealed, including sugar, flour, rice and beans. If you open a bag of chips, I give you full license to eat the entire bag, they will be soggy the next morning. (Really, you don't eat chips in the morning? Your loss.) Baking in high altitude and moisture brings a new meaning to the "Is it done yet?" question. It is not a fix and forget type of kitchen, you'll have to be constantly checking on it.

So you get two different extremes of the spectrum, the moist and the Sahara. How you manage both will have your family thanking you!

21. MOMMA ARE WE GONNA STARVE ON THIS MOUNTAIN?

There is nothing worse than children complaining they are starving to death while it is taking forever getting a meal on the table. This is something to keep in consideration when cooking on Beech Mountain. Remember instructions on boxes have a separate "high altitude" instruction. That is because cooking and baking are different above 3,000 feet and Beech Mountain is over 5,000 feet.

Why? In a nutshell, cooking and baking all revolve around the boiling point of water, and the higher the altitude, the lower the boiling point of water. Without going into atmospheric pressure and time and space continuum and who exactly is Luke Skywalker's father, it simply takes longer for water to boil, so it takes longer for things to cook. As for baking, water evaporates more quickly at a higher altitude so most recipes call for extra liquid while others decrease the sugar and baking powder.

So, if you are going to the Christmas party during the winter or the BBQ during the summer, don't be surprised if many of the baked goods are either dry and cracked on the top, or the cakes have fallen in, it's just an accepted science on the mountain. Always use the high altitude directions and remember, start cooking early. It is painful when someone chews off your arm due to hunger because potatoes are taking forever to boil.

When vacationing or living on Beech Mountain, we discussed high altitude, now you need understanding of "mountain living" or getting from here to there. This means, it is not an easy or quick drive to the grocery story if you forgot an ingredient for your Bloody Mary. Here on Beech Mountain, we have Fred's General Mercantile, who's motto is, "If we don't have it, you don't need it." They have that forgotten item in a pinch, everything from local bloody mary mix or that much needed ball peen hammer, and of course beer and wine.

There are two chain grocery stores off of Beech Mountain, a Food Lion and Lowes, along with a Dollar General in Banner Elk almost qualifying as a third. These are great resources for staples prior to traveling up the mountain. I always make that stop before climbing Beech Mountain, no matter how tired I am, because once you are on the mountain, you do not leave the mountain (I'll explain this later.) Make your vacation list prior to traveling to Beech Mountain and save yourself time and money with a stop there.

Back to grocery store planning before you travel up Beech Mountain Parkway. There are two different types, winter and other seasons.

Winter - did I mention that Beech Mountain gets over 84 inches of snow a season? And did I mention it takes time to clear the roads because usually a bunch of tourists from Florida are stuck because they don't know how to drive in the snow? If you want to navigate the switchbacks of Beech Mountain frequently, you can go back to the "I'll go to the store when I need it" type of shopping. Me? I plan for at least two weeks worth of meals, then do my grocery shopping. I buy family packs of meat, using them in several recipes over different meals, not only stretching my dollar but saving gas and time not having to leave the mountain as often during winter. Many homes also keep a chest freezer in their basement for this very purpose. I always keep frozen vegetables and fruits in my freezer during the winter, combating the possibility of scurvy in my home when I cannot get off the mountain to the grocery store due to snow. I have one friend who plans her meals to a science, only having to leave the mountain once a month for groceries and gas. Truly talented! I, on the other hand after only one experience of sliding down the mountain on E because I forgot groceries and to fill the tank, always refill both when it hits the halfway point.

You'll also notice when you know people on the mountain, a trip to the grocery store becomes a community event. You'll put the call out that you are venturing off the mountain and after much communication from your tribe after your normal trip to the grocery store, you'll add motor oil, diapers, jock itch creme, several cases of beer and of course, a case of wine.

Other seasons - once the winter weather closes for good, usually by Mid-April, a trip to the grocery store in Banner Elk is not such a monumental journey. Another perk is the market on fresh produce opens up. There are several produce stands in Banner Elk. Once the summer season hits downtown Banner Elk hosts a Farmer's Market one day a week. One of the benefits of living in the mountains is the cooler weather of summer. Cooler weather means produce ripens more slowly than in the foothills or Piedmont. So if you are thinking about going strawberry or blueberry picking, call ahead and check, make sure the fruit has ripened enough.

If you are into local, natural honey, Beech Mountain Beekeeping has a store on the backside of the mountain, and several local farms sell honey at the produce stands or by the side of the road. Fred's General Mercantile also sells local honey. I've always said my allergies became manageable when I started ingesting local honey on a daily basis. This gives my body the pollen of local flowers and creates an immunity making allergy season much easier.

Fred's is open all year round for those last minute items. Fred's also has a great video rental section, giving families something to do if it is raining on Beech Mountain. Pickup what you need either in Banner Elk or on Beech Mountain and enjoy a beautiful evening in front of the fire or outside in front of the BBQ, all because you planned ahead.

22. IS HE TALKING TO ME or HELLO THERE!

Either on your first trip to Beech Mountain, or your 40th year of living here, there are two types of people on the mountain. Those who wave and those who don't wave.

Those who wave are a very jolly lot, happy to be on the mountain in the cool summer breeze demonstrating it by showing appreciation to everyone they see. This starts in the car. When driving the roads of Beech Mountain, keep your right hand free from the steering wheel because you will spend a lot of time waving back to people you do not know. This includes the driver in the other car just being courteous, the walker by the side of the road making sure you see them, as well as your kids chasing behind the car because you forgot them. "We's all family on Beech Mountain," means we expect everyone to be courteous, and that means wave.

Non wavers usually are not from the area. If they move here and don't wave after the first few weeks, someone will explain to them waving is expected on Beech Mountain. An elderly friend came to visit. We were driving down to the Beech Mountain Club pool and he was clearly violating the wave policy of the mountain. "Why are all these people waving to me? I don't know any of them," he muttered, his hands staying at 10 and 2 on the steering wheel navigating the winding roads. "They are trying to be friendly," I answered back, waving for him, figuring if they saw me wave, the sentiment was expressed keeping both of us in good standing. "They need to go wave to someone else," he muttered driving his 15 miles per hour. These non-wavers usually come from up North, where everyone isn't family in a small given area. They think someone waving means they want to rob you, so they gun the engine and continue on.

Another non-waver is the new driver to Beech Mountain. They are so busy trying to navigate the switchbacks while not hitting other drivers, adding in a wave is just beyond their ability. I was in the car with a new driver, explaining the wave policy. His face turned white, prompting me to add, "Don't wave, I'll do it for you. Just keep your hands at 10 and 2." So if you wave to someone and they don't wave back, along with the deer in the headlights look, just figure they are trying to avoid a collision with you, quite possibly saving your life.

Some wavers are very enthusiastic. One example during the summer season is the senior citizen. If you see them waving at you in a panic, don't worry. You can still stop and ask if they are having a heart attack, but you'll find the reason they are waving is for you to "SLOW DOWN!" It doesn't matter if you are doing 20 or 8 miles per hour, it will be too fast for this poor soul walking his little dog. Just wave back at him and move along on your merry way.

The other type of enthusiastic wavers are the people that actually know you. Believe me, the longer you stay on Beech Mountain, the more people will know you. It will go from the casual acquaintance to the, "I saw your red 2013 Acura with the dent on the right front panel in the parking lot of the restaurant, thought I'd come in and say hello." No really, they will know the car you drive, the color of the clothes you wear on the ski slopes, and the color of your yoga mat for exercise class. If they are waving enthusiastically, just do the same because you probably do know them, you just haven't seen them yet without their goggles. Some wavers are so enthusiastic they bang on the windows of their house as you walk by, or as you ski by expecting a just as enthusiastic wave back.

Which brings me to the friendliness of this small mountain town, "We's all family on the mountain," means everyone is family when it comes to Beech Mountain. One epic family story involves a local legend, who I invited over to dinner after skiing on the slopes. I never saw him that night, figuring he got a better offer. However the next day he was screaming at me from the lift chair, telling me to stop and wait right there for him. He came flying down the hill with this story:

"You're not going to believe it. I went over to your house last night."
"What? I didn't see you."
"Hold on. I went in took my shoes off leaving them by the door like everyone else. I am polite like that. I grabbed a beer from the fridge, cracked it open, sat on the sofa for the football game before looking around. Then I thought, 'Who are these people?' I didn't recognize a soul."
"What?"
"I was in the wrong house!" he said, laughing.
"What happened?" I asked.
"Well, they invited me to dinner." He said matter of factly.
Of course, we're on Beech Mountain. "What did you do?" I asked, incredulous.

"I stayed and ate."

So if you want to be part of Beech Mountain family, practice your waves. Your prom waves, your wrestler tap outs, to simply the "I don't know you but I've read here that you are supposed to wave" waves, we're all family on the mountain and you may just get a free meal out of it.

23. AMENITIES FROM TOP TO BOTTOM

Beech Mountain offers so much more than just a ski resort. Many don't realize Beech Mountain is a year round destination. If you haven't been to the mountain, or are just discovering the other seasons of Beech, there are a number of great places for a fun Spring/Summer/Fall day.

Beech Mountain Bark Park - Many people ask, why a Bark Park when you have an entire mountain as a playground? The concept of the Beech Mountain Bark Park was an area for dogs to play and exercise without endangering themselves or the beautiful wildlife of the mountain. The park opened in 2012, as a community project with the joint efforts of The Town of Beech Mountain and Beech Mountain Club.

What does a Bark Park offer? Two separate areas based on the size of the dog. Each area has natural landscaping, is completely fenced, with agility features. Add in water stations, tennis balls, the "Do Do" stations, and dogs can run and play while owners sit and chat at the picnic tables and park benches. A nice addition to the Park is its location along the Beech Mountain Greenway Trail making a nice walk a great way to end play in the park. The Beech Mountain Bark Park is located in the upper corner of the "Kite Field" across from Beech Mountain Town Hall. Even if you don't have a dog, take a nice stroll along the field and watch all the antics of the Bark Park, owners and dogs alike.

Coffey Lake is located off of Lake Road below the Beech Mountain Club's tennis courts, pool and fitness center. This spot, unknown to winter visitors, is a small lake stocked with fish,and has a nice walking trail around it. Beech Mountain Club offers canoe rentals at the lake for club members. If you want something a little more challenging than walking around the lake, follow the gravel road to a dead end the Pond Creek Trails. Take Lower Pond Creek for a strenuous hike to a beautiful waterfall or Upper Pond Creek following the stream with bridges, rhododendrons, and a more moderate trail. Reminder - when fishing anywhere on Beech Mountain, make sure you have your fishing license. Fred's General Mercantile sells them.

Buckeye Lake is 5 miles beyond town on the back side of Beech Mountain. This is a larger lake than Coffey Lake also offering fishing. Buckeye Recreation Center located on the hill above the lake offers free canoe rentals, a paddle boat and fishing poles. This lake is also stocked, and has several picnic shelters along the shoreline for a great day on the lake. Genesis Wildlife Rehabilitation was located at the building at the base. You'll still see some of the cages left when they moved out. Most of the animals were relocated to Lees McRae College. The building is now a private residence. A quick trip to May Rehabilitation Center off of Hickory Nut Gap Road in Banner Elk visiting the animals is well worth the trip.

Buckeye Recreation Center located at 1330 Pineridge Road is part of the Town of Beech Mountain. This indoor facility houses a gymnasium, a tennis court and basketball court, indoor walking track, fitness room with equipment, group exercise room, meeting rooms and free wifi in the lobby. Visitors to Beech Mountain can pay a per visit fee, or a monthly or yearly fee for using the facility. Buckeye Recreation Center offers group exercise classes year round, with more classes offered in the summer season than over winter. Look to Buckeye for family fun events from Halloween to a Holiday themed Yule Log celebration during the Winter Season to Outdoors Camp for the kids during the summer season. Rentals for Buckeye Lake are also located at the Recreation Center.

Outdoor options at Buckeye Recreation Center include a football field, playground, and walking trail. The playground is a tree house enthusiast's dream with rope courses, made of large logs of cedar and plenty of relaxing picnic tables for child watching. If you spy a wooden trellis while walking the trail around the field, make a side journey down the trail to Buckeye Falls. You'll be glad you did.

Emerald Mountain Outback is to me, an avid hiker/biker a crown jewel of Beech Mountain. Maintained by the Buckeye Recreation Center, these 8 miles of mountain bike/hiking trails are an outdoor enthusiasts dream. From grunting up Grunt Hill to the beautiful views of Pride Rock and Elk River Valley Rock, this is the perfect place to disappear from the world for a while. We always joke, wondering why only one view on the trail gained the name "Awesome" when all three Southern Ridge Views are awesome. You can access the Emerald Mountain Outback by following Pinnacle Ridge Rd which is almost a continuation of Beech Mountain Parkway, up to the top of the mountain to the Parking Lot, you can't miss the signs for Emerald Outback. I always tell friends to take a picture of the trail system with their phone. That way we're not sending out the search parties after dark looking for you. Better yet, pick up a free Emerald Outback map at the Chamber of Commerce or Fred's General Mercantile. Oh, and if you are on your mountain bike, remember the difference between the front and back brakes - one will send you over the handlebars if you use it on a downhill. This never happened to me, I'm telling you this for a friend.

Thanks to the Town of Beech Mountain, children can sled on the **sledding hill** during the winter season at no charge. Just bring your own equipment and helmets. I have found other places on the mountain less crowded and a little bit steeper but locals are begging me not to tell you where!

I must mention the extensive **trail system of Beech Mountain**, trails for hiking, biking, snow shoeing, cross country skiing or pitching your hammock and letting the day go. An entire book could outline the over 20 miles of trails on the mountain, but your best bet is to visit the Town of Beech Mountain website for trails, difficulty, distance and directions. (www.townofbeechmountain.com) or you could break the bank, buying a $1.00 trail map at Fred's or the Chamber of Commerce. I've hidden mentions in this book of my favorites, see if you can find them, then hike them and I'll guarantee you'll love them as much as I do.

There's so much more than just the snow on Beech Mountain. An off season trip during summer brings high temps of the 70's and low temps in the 50's. A trip in the autumn brings the spectacular colors of fall in the mountains and a trip in the spring shows nature's promise as the valley is in bloom while Beech is slowly moving out of winter. I always say, one of the joys of living on a mountain is you can visit the lowlands during the start of a spring season, then go back up the mountain and experience the season again. It's a win/win situation.

24. MEMBERSHIP HAS ITS PRIVILEGES - THE BEECH MOUNTAIN CLUB

Beech Mountain Club is a mostly summer venue on the mountain. With amenities geared toward the golfer and to the family, it is a wonderful asset for summer living or summer vacation. Let me outline some of the benefits of being a member.

The clubhouse and dining room are located facing the backside of the mountain with amazing views of North Carolina, Tennessee and Virginia. Open 5 days a week through summer season, June - Labor Day, the clubhouse features specialties each night, Crazy 8's or $8 dollar dinners, Two for Tuesday - Two Salads/Soups and two entrees to the Prime Rib buffet and Sportsman Buffet, and open menu nights. This year we enjoyed the Fireman's Ball in July at the Clubhouse. For a donation to the Fire Department, you are invited to a dinner dance. The food was spectacular, the open bar made everyone happy and we danced the night away - all for a good cause. Visit www.beechmountainvfd.org for your donation. This is a summer event not to be missed.

Other great summertime amenities with a club membership include:

Tennis Courts - the 10 Har-Tru courts play host to leagues, junior leagues and lessons. If you are not a tennis player, sitting and watching the tournaments from the grand stands is the perfect way to spend a Saturday afternoon. These tournaments are often followed by a friendly chicken/covered dish supper.

Golf course - the Beech Mountain Club Golf course, 18 ridge top holes boasts magnificent views of North Carolina, Virginia and Tennessee. Originally designed by William Byrd, the recent renovation by renowned golf architect Tom Jackson extended the course to 6,250 feet. Elevation on the course ranges from 4,200 to 4,700 feet, along with practice facilities, a pro shop and driving range. The Fairway Cafe located by the clubhouse is a great casual venue for a quick bite to eat before or after you hit the golf course. You can always sit outside on the clubhouse deck enjoying after play cocktails.

Pool - the pool is located off of Lake Road is equipped with a pool house and a small splash park with zero entry for the little ones. The best part of the pool is it is heated to 85 degrees. Sometimes on that cool June day, you'll see everyone sitting in the pool with the water up to their noses. There is a bathhouse with showers and towels are provided by the club on weekends. The lap lanes are an excellent way to exercise. Just remember you are above 5,000 feet so don't feel down if after few laps it feels like you're hacking out half a lung. The Pumphouse Grill located at the pool, is open on the weekends and sells cafe style food and beverages. You can bring your own picnic to the pool, but no glassware is allowed.

The biggest summertime savior on the mountain is the **Beech Mountain Club Day Camp**, running June and July at the Pavilion and Pool. Parents or Grandparents drop off children at 9AM, coming back to pick them up at 330PM or scheduling after camp golf, tennis or swimming lessons even later. Yes, if you have grandchildren visiting, this keeps them busy and gives you a little peace. The camp also offers Parents Night Out, sleepovers at the pavilion, and day trips for the older children to ropes courses, water parks, etc.

Applications for the camp are found in the Administration office or online. Go for that little slice of heaven, a mountain vacation everyone enjoys, even the kids at CAMP!

Fitness Center is located also off of Lakeledge Road, with weight machines, treadmills, ellipticals, free weights etc. Personal Trainers are available. In 2015 a new Fitness Room opened filling summers with classes ranging from Stretch, Tone and Balance to Barre and Cross Training. You'll need a membership card for the Fitness Center, which is obtained from the Administration Office.

Pickleball Courts - Did you know there is a US Pickleball Association? Created in 1965 by 3 Dads on the Bainbridge Ferry from Seattle, Pickleball combines tennis, ping-pong and badminton. The court is the size of a badminton court, Beech Mountain Club's three courts are located outside next to the pool. The club sponsors Pickleball Tournaments along with Pickleball Coaches during the summer helping you master the game. Paddles and balls are available through the Pickleball Center.

Alpen Haus is located behind the Lodge of Beech Mountain Resort, offers an alternative for club members for food and drink. The resort can get pretty busy on a Saturday, so having a place with games, great food and lockers for members is an added plus. There is also parking available at the Alpen Haus, with the slopes a short walk away.

During the winter months, the club is still active with pot luck dinners, field trips, a book club, bible studies, and limited exercise classes at the fitness center. Contact Administration and join our 3 Seasons Club newsletters for all these activities.

There are so many activities during the summer for Beech Mountain Club members, you'll have to look for the weekly bulletins for the skinny. I've been to a moonshine tasting, taught a class called "Facebook for Grandparents," enjoyed an art lecture luncheon and hiked with the club on many trails.

Looking for pictures of the Beech Mountain Club? Check out www.beechmountainclub.org all the information is available there, including how to become a member.

Membership does have its privileges!

25. SUMMERTIME AT BEECH MOUNTAIN RESORT

Many locals on Beech Mountain mourn the last day of ski season, tearing up on that last chairlift ride to the top.

Others look forward to the next chairlift ride---

With a bicycle!

Beech Mountain Resort reopens as Beech Mountain Bike Park for summer downhill mountain biking from Memorial Weekend through Labor Day Weekend. After a much needed break for Spring, the resort is ready to go with all kinds of activities for summer!

Beech Mountain Bike Park offers 6 downhill mountain biking trails from beginner to advanced with chairlift access to the top. These trails, designed by professionals, are maintained by a park crew all summer. Bike rentals are available in the village along with lessons for beginners. Beech Mountain Bike Park offers mountain biking clinics, along with ladies days and specials for mountain biking. Make sure you are well padded riding see Protect That Biggest Asset. Information is available through their website.

Summer signals the reopening of the Beech Mountain Brewery, Beechtree Bar and Grille and 5506' SkyBar. A mile high summer concert series can't be beat. Concerts take place at the 5506 bar customers enjoying outdoor music in the clouds. Concerts run every Saturday afternoon through the summer season. Plan on arriving early for live music as everyone always waits until the last minute and lift line can be long getting to the top. Lift Tickets are available through

Ski Beech Sports running a single round trip. Take in the scenery as you ascend to the top!

Mile High Yoga runs every Saturday and Sunday at 5506' and is open to all ages and all levels. Nothing like a photo at the top after a yoga session, or a cold beverage as the SkyBar opens at the conclusion of yoga. Lift ticket and class fee as well as yoga mat rentals are through Ski Beech Sports. If you choose to hike up to the top for class, you can pay cash for the class to the instructor. Every August, Beech Mountain Resort hosts Alivenfest, a three day yoga festival, with events planned all over the mountain. Find details on yoga and Alivenfest at www.beechmountainresort.com

Beech Mountain Resort offers Disc Golf, with two different courses available based on ability. Take the lift tot the top and make a day of it or hike halfway and enjoy the outdoors with friends.

All activities start and end in the Village at the base of the lift. Summer lift tickets are one round trip to the top. So stay and enjoy as long as you like making sure you hit the lift before the last rider down. Ski Patrol usually rolls through the 5506 Skybar letting everyone know time is running out. If you miss the last chair, you can always hike down the slopes.

In the Village, enjoy an ice cold Beech Mountain Brewery Beer with friends, sitting outside in the sun or enjoy a casual meal in the BeechTree Bar and Grille.

There is no parking at the top for 5506' SkyBar or yoga. Arrive early, buy a lift ticket and enjoy the ride to the top. You can stay as long as you like at the top. Some take the lift to the top enjoying the scenery then hike down the slopes.

Some visitors park at Emerald Mountain Outback Bike Trails and hike up to the 5506' Skybar for the concert series. Exercise is always good for you!

You may also catch a few of the downhill races at the resort during the summer. Ask any patroller in a red vest for the best vantage point and watch why this sport is such an adrenaline rush.

26. THE HISTORY - OFFICIAL AND UNOFFICIAL OF BEECH MOUNTAIN

Starting in 1967 with the opening of Beech Mountain Ski Resort, there are so many stories on this mountain that you will never grow bored. Don't have a local resident willing to play storyteller for you? Then stop by the Beech Mountain Museum, located next to Fred's General Mercantile on top of Beech Mountain.

Starting with the Cherokees, the first visitors to the mountain, the museum moves to the lives of early settlers on the mountain, and the famous Keller-Presnell cemetery. There are memories of the first Tour de Pont, a huge bicycling race up Beech Mountain, now relived through the annual Beech Mountain Metric. Memorabilia from the Land of Oz, the Carolina Caribbean Corporation and of course Beech Mountain Resort are on display in the museum. In 2015, Beech Mountain Resort reopened the Red Baron Room, starting a new era, stop by the museum, view the history of the room prior to your first trip to the resort.

Little known facts found at the museum: Lower and Upper Pond Creek hikes were once part of the path of a narrow gauge logging rail road in the late 1920's. You can still find a remanent remaining on Upper Pond Creek.

And where Buckeye Recreation Center is located, it was a labor camp for the logging workers on the mountain.

The Beech Mountain Historical Society created a pictorial book on the history of Beech Mountain, for sale in the Beech Mountain Museum. Also look for an annual picture calendar created by the Artist Guild of Beech Mountain, it the museum's primary fundraiser.

The museum is staffed by volunteers, you can visit when you see a sign outside the blue building beside Fred's General Mercantile saying, "Museum Open Today" it is worth the trip to see the history of the mountain we call home. Oh, and it is free, although donations are always welcome.

Good places for a little history/gossip on the mountain? You can get the official story from the Beech Mountain Museum or you can get the unofficial story, along with several amazing anecdotes from longtime locals on the mountain. Where do these reclusive people hide on the mountain? A few good places:

Fast Eddies, 1005 Beech Mountain Parkway. Eddies, which started as a hot dog stand on the mountain, serves hot dogs, BBQ, pizza and good side dish of local lore. You'll still catch a few "old timers" sitting at the bar talking about the good old days. Better yet with the purchase of a few beers, they'll bend your ear for quite a while, that is, until someone comes in hearing a story about them being told and puts the cab-ash on it.

Beechtree Bar & Grille - located in the Alpine Village of Beech Mountain Resort, this is the venue of choice of long timers, usually after getting a few runs in on the snow, then retiring for a few drinks and some food. These locals, as they are still on the snow, may start their conversations about replaced knees, and hips, and broken arms, but will soon move into the time Grand Mariner sponsored a race at Beech Mountain back in the day when the bartenders didn't really know what Grand Mariner was and were pouring pint glasses full for the patrons. I'll just leave that one there.

"5506" is good for old timers, only early in the morning. Years of being on the snow makes them realize you do not combine drinking with putting on skis to get back down the mountain. That is why the majority of them end up at the Beechtree Bar and Grille at the bottom. Best sighting place of the local legend? At the bar in the corner, back to the wall, away from the crowd, real estate preserved.

Ski Patrol - many patrollers on the mountain have been working the snow since they were younguns. Unfortunately, the only real way of hanging out with Ski Patrol is getting hurt, so we'll just skip that one right now.

The Lift Line - on some busy days you'll spend a little time hanging out in the lift line. If you spot someone in a 1980's fart bag (translation one piece zip up ski suit) and it is not the fabulous 80's weekend at the resort, they're an old timer. Try hanging out by them, listening it to their, "I remember the day when…." conversations.

Riding the Lift, you'll have a five minute ride, you will be surprised at what you can learn riding the lift. If the person looks interesting, skip the "where are you from" conversation and ask directly how long they've been at the resort. They will revel you with stories of the hay days and odd characters of the resort.

You will find the unofficial story just as, if not more than, entertaining than the official story, listening to both sides will not only keep you in the know about the mountain, but give you plenty of fodder for stories when you are riding the lift.

27. YOU ARE EITHER HIGH OR NOT!

When visiting or living on Beech Mountain, there is only one place that interests you, being on the mountain. Anywhere else is "off the mountain." Off the mountain means trekking out of the wilderness into the unknown, a place making many year round residents of Beech Mountain quake in their boots.

Not only does leaving the mountain involve navigating Beech Mountain Parkway, it also includes navigating the local tourists; those in tire chains during a sunny winter day or riding their brakes so hard going down the mountain that a cloud of black smoke follows them. Ask a resident if they want to meet you off the mountain, they'll tell you it is not worth it. I remember the first time I invited a resident of Beech Mountain to Banner Elk for a light lunch in a local restaurant, saying, "We'll just pop down for lunch and be back in no time."

She looked at me as if I'd lost my mind. Opened her mouth, closing it, looking at me again replying, "Going off the mountain?" Of course before coming to Beech Mountain, I was used to driving thirty minutes to the mall to get my teenager that "certain" pair of jeans, so leaving the mountain didn't sound so daunting, "Yeah? Why?" She gave me a look like she was second guessing her decision of friending me before replying, "Let's just go up to the Beech Alpen Inn, it is close."

Now that I am living on the mountain, I've contracted the same disease disabling locals on Beech Mountain from passing the "Gear Down for Safety" sign before you start your descent. Called, "Lowlandophobia" or fear of the low lands, this disease causes nausea and anxiety if altitude dips below 5,000 feet above sea level. I remember wondering if cutting up our last grape four ways qualified as the fruit quotient of the day so I didn't have to leave the mountain for groceries. I was saved anxiety by finding apple sauce in the pantry, calling that the fruit of the day.

Lowlandophobics are not afraid of the lowlands per say, we just see that as another part of the world, far away from our home mountain.

Some brave souls have conquered Lowlandophobia. If you are one of them, keep your poor high friends in mind. Put out the APB when you plan a trip past the "Gear down for safety" sign. You'll be inundated by calls, texts, emails of picking up "just a few things." Consider it taking one for the mountain when everyone in the local grocery store is staring at your purchases of Jock Itch creme, baby formula, milk, chocolate bars, and of course a case of beer. Your neighbors will thank you.

What is the difference between a Beech Mountain resident and a Lowlander?

Low landers have boots AND shoes. Beech Mountain residents have hiking boots and snow boots. Lowlanders have the Imelda Marcos closet full of shoes, because living where it doesn't snow means you can actually break out the cute shoes and wear them on a dinner date. Some beg to differ with this opinion, because you CAN wear cute shoes on Beech Mountain during the winter time. You simply wear your snow boots to the venue, carry your cute shoes in your purse, leave the snow boots by the door throwing on the cute shoes. Then of course you realize you left something in the car so you put the snow boots back on traveling out to the car, then back to the venue, changing shoes again. You see my point here, after attempting this several times, like most Beech Mountain residents, your cute shoes will mold in the closet until you have an opportunity to travel "off the mountain" then you'll break them out.

Low landers do not worry about gas. I don't know how many friends travel all the way up Beech Mountain, arrive at my house saying, "Man, I'm on E, I'll have to get gas on the way down." Do you realize that you may get stuck in your car in the snow and E is not going to help you? Residents always make sure the tank is full, unless we are broke. Of course every once in a long while we forget. Lowlanders don't know our secret, but there is a way of surfing your way down Beech Mountain Parkway on "E" and actually making it to the Exon station in Banner Elk without the engine quitting. Some secrets stay safe until someone offers the right amount of money.

Low landers think in the moment. The "oh, I didn't pick up any groceries, I'll just run out now," still works for them. They can travel to the grocery for that one item they forgot. Those of us on the mountain will possibly venture out to Fred's General Mercantile for that ingredient if we REALLY need it (Fred's Motto: "If we don't have it, you don't need it") Or we will scour for the perfect substitution for soy bean curd. Better yet, those with Lowlandophobia plan out the week in meals, because that trip to the grocery store is a "journey." You have to commit to going to the store, you can't just pop by. You can pop by Fred's for that missed item but beware, you may come out with nutmeg, a new pair of hiking boots, a soft sweater AND a pair of skis!

How can you help a Beech Mountain resident with "lowlandophobia?" Take them on a trip to Florida when Beech Mountain is still in a deep freeze, letting them bask in the sun in a sundress normally meant for Beech Mountain in

August. The next time you offer a lunch in Banner Elk, they may actually follow you off the mountain, not for the promise of free food, because since they never leave the mountain, they may not know the way.

Or better yet, invite them somewhere and offer your services as chauffeur, it's very easy to conquer a disease when someone else is driving for you.

28. WORD TRAVELS FAST

There will be different stories about different people on the mountain. It is best wait until you meet them before determining the truth. We had a Gnarnia festival on the mountain several years ago, involving psychedelic characters, music, camping and other what not. Don't believe a word from anyone on those stories, most of the locals left town that weekend for a break from the crowds. Everything else is here-say.

You can make up your own stories, and you can listen to all the stories of years gone by, which would make a great book. Sit back and relax with friends remembering that "what happens on the mountain, stays on the mountain."

Did you hear that? It is gossip traveling on the mountain.

Go ahead a read this to Dem Bones song:

Someone gossiped dem mountain bones,
Someone gossiped den mountain bones,
Someone gossiped dem mountain bones,
Now hear how the word travels fast!

The story got told on the lift bone,
Then word traveled down to the ticket booth bone,
The ticket booth bone connected it to the shuttle bus bone,
Moving it over to the Pinnacle bone.

Some one told some one else at the Pinnacle pool bone,

Helping it travel out to the Fred's breakfast bone.
Someone put their paper down to hear it correctly,
Taking it out and over to the dump bone.

Dat gossip, dat gossip gonna walk around,
Dat gossip, dat gossip gonna walk around.
Dat gossip, dat gossip gonna walk around,
Now hear how word travels fast!

Dat word traveled out of the dump bone,
Moving quickly down to the Bullwinkles bone.
Passed with a pizza at the Alpen bone,
Stopping by Eddies for a hot dog passing the bone.

The bone left Eddies moving down to the pool bone,
Where someone asked if it was really true.
No answer was given so it traveled over to the Fitness
Center bone,
Making a quick stop at the Pickleball court bone.
Dat bone then traveled back up to Alpen again,
Then casually mentioned at Buckeye bone.

Dat gossip, dat gossip gonna walk around,
Dat gossip, dat gossip gonna walk around.
Dat gossip, dat gossip gonna walk around,
Now hear how word travels fast!

Finally, the word started down the mountain,
But didn't make it past the Jackalopes bone,
Word does travel fast
But it usually doesn't leave pass the first switchback

Dat gossip, dat gossip gonna walk around,
Dat gossip, dat gossip gonna walk around.
Dat gossip, dat gossip gonna walk around,
Now hear how word travels fast!

29. CHRISTMAS ON THE MOUNTAIN

Everyone knows the major holiday on Beech Mountain is Christmas! Christmas falls right during Winter Break, a sweet term for the two weeks kids are off from school prompting road tripping, getting that SKI trip in! Our resort over Winter Break grows by over 15 thousand people, and most of them are on the ski slopes.

How do you have a successful Winter Holiday on Beech Mountain? It is easy! Start with the natural decorations on the mountain provided by Mother Nature! Snow! There is no better way of getting in the mood for the holidays than a blanket of snow on the ground. On Beech Mountain, with over 84 inches of fresh snow annually, a majority of our Christmas holidays involve snow on the ground. Being a Southern community, we do have the occasional rain during Christmas even one year freezing rain blowing out the electric on the mountain. Residents and visitors waited for Mountain Electric Cooperative coming to the rescue, prompting many of us to get creative with the Christmas dinner. Did you know Prime Rib tastes amazing grilled for a day outside in the freezing rain? There was even enough gas left for sautéing vegetables and boiling water for mashed potatoes.

If you are a Christmas type, one of the benefits of being in Western North Carolina is the Fraser Fir tree Industry. This is one of the largest holiday industries with 20% of all Christmas trees in the state coming from our High Country Farms. Many families have this sweet picture in mind about a Christmas tree, just as I did my first year on Beech Mountain. I saw my family marching out on a crisp winter morning, singing Christmas carols as we walked through the fields looking for the perfect tree. I should have known that things would not go as planned when we ended up at Horney Hollow Christmas Tree Farm.

"What do you mean going out looking for a tree? Let's just buy one at the grocery store," the family whines.

"This is our Christmas tradition, let's make this family memory," I reply.

"But do you notice it is snowing outside?" They all ask together.

"That will make it even prettier when we walk through the fields looking for our tree," I grit out.

They realize they already lost the argument when I formed that perfect picture in my mind, we were going for a tree. What also didn't help was the soft snow turned into driving snow as we pulled into the farm, so much snow that Mr. Horney, (yes, that was his name) looked up surprised when we blew into his office, almost extinguishing his fire.

"You are going out there?"

I nodded. Getting a tree was an item on my to do list. I was going to accomplish this even if hell froze over. With the amount of snow, I was beginning to wonder. "Yes, we are," I replied

"Well," he said with a long pause, you could almost see the *they must be insane* thought going through his mind. "Go find your tree then I'll come out and cut it down." Translation, "You go out there and freeze to death, I'll find you come spring."

We left Mr. Horney warm and cozy in his office, marching through the sideways snow. Every tree I stopped by, the family went crazy at "how perfect" the tree was, even if it was simply a stick poking out of the ground. I know they were just saying this to get back to the warm cozy office, but I wanted the perfect tree. It took another 15 minutes of listening to my children complain of the frostbite on their toes before I found the tree. We marched back to Mr. Horney who informed us we had to follow him back to the tree. He'll cut it down but we continue down memory lane dragging it back to the truck. Luckily with the wind during the blizzard all I saw was my children's mouths moving, I couldn't hear their complaining. I did make a memory, each year I bring up getting a tree they immediately remember how cold it was that day.

If you have Lowlandaphobia (see You Are Either High Or Not) and don't want to leave the mountain, Fred's General Mercantile has a Christmas Tree Farm on the mountain, tucked back on his farm. The trees are reasonable, beautiful and just a short drive away. Are you sensing the theme of Fred's General Mercantile, they do live up to their motto, "If we don't have it, you don't need it."

Don't have time to cut down a tree as you are on vacation? Little known fact, you can have a tree delivered from Fred's General Mercantile Christmas Tree Farm for a fee. I called and asked if someone could deliver a tree into the stand in my living while we were gone. I was too busy to get over to the tree farm, and how much fun telling my small children our "Christmas Elf" Hanz delivered the tree from the North Pole. "We're on it," the staff at Fred's said, excited about putting up a tree in an elf's name. When we came home later that night, we found the fattest, most pregnant tree ever, sitting in the middle of our small living room. I cringed looking at the 5lbs of glitter forming elf tracks from the back door, up my carpeted steps ending right at the tree. I couldn't stay angry as though my son held his little brother back, exclaiming, "Don't touch that, it is elf pee!" Fred's General Mercantile saved me sneaking out in the middle of the night, probably in a blowing snow storm finding a tree.

Santa loves to visit Beech Mountain. Beech Mountain Ski Resort holds regular "Pictures with Santa" visits during the holiday break. Local hotels offer breakfast with Santa, while Buckeye Recreation Center offers Breakfast with Santa and Mrs. Claus. Fred's General Mercantile also has a "Visit with Santa" at the Gazebo outside the store, and local hotels also have a few Santa sightings. On a crisp winter day with snow on the ground there is nothing better that a discussion with Santa to get you into the Christmas Spirit.

Other winter holiday fun includes Hayrides on the mountain singing Christmas Carols. Buckeye Recreation Center offers a "Yule Log" bonfire with hot cocoa, s'mores and the fixings. Local High Country towns celebrate the winter holidays with special tree lighting ceremonies, making the towns look magical. Add in the snowstorms of winter and many a Christmas morning, there is a good chance you could wake up to a beautiful White Christmas.

30. HOLIDAYS ON BEECH MOUNTAIN

New Years Eve on Beech Mountain is celebrated at Beech Mountain Resort. The Beechtree Bar and Grille hosts a New Year's party with live music, food and of course a lot of dancing. Night snow enthusiasts enjoy time on the slopes, finishing the last day of the year in the Grille waiting for the countdown. Weather permitting, as with anything on Beech Mountain, fireworks celebrate the New Year with the best vantage point outside at the base of the slopes watching them explode over head.

Several restaurants in the area offer New Year's parties, most involving live music, and all kinds of party favors. If you are not the late night type, or simply want to spend the last day of the year with your family, then light a fire and enjoy a glass of champagne. Or you can do what my boys did one year, bang pots so hard at the stroke of midnight they dented the metal! Nothing cooks evenly ever since!

Valentine's Day

Valentine's Day is still during the snow season at Beech Mountain. You can enjoy a romantic Valentine's dinner at any of the local restaurants without leaving the mountain. (see "Lowlandophobia" or You Are Either High Or Not) Many locals to the mountain take any chance to hit the slopes, even if it means leaving a rose on the kitchen table as you venture out for the first chair. The resort even has some type of event for the holiday, Speed Chairlift Dating is once example.

Last Day of Season

Sometime in March, weather permitting, Beech Mountain Resort will hold an end of season party on the resort. Different years included the sport of "Pond Skimming" where you attempt to ski or board across a pond of frozen water. My favorite part of this is "Pond Watching" or placing bets with friends on who's not going to make it and the awesomeness of their crash or yardsale (see slopes lingo.) Some years have included a BBQ for patrons, or a day just for the season pass holders. You can always check the resort's website for up to date information.

I put the Last Day of Season as a holiday just for the fun of the resort. For all of us ski bums it starts our " extended mourning" period, lasting from Mid-March to end of November. We usually end up chasing the "Spring Snow," traveling to other area resorts if they are still open, taking a few turns on what has not melted, traveling out West taking advantage of late season specials and springtime snow. One year we went to Utah the first week of April. It snowed every day! Other times, it was a nice slushfest by midday but any day on the snow is a good day.

Easter

Beech Mountain pretty much goes into hibernation for spring. Residents working at the resorts take much needed vacations, businesses close for a break and lack of visitors. Many local Banner Elk, Boone and surrounding area churches offer Easter services, and the Beech Mountain Club will sometimes schedule a brunch at the club house. My family enjoys a sunrise service on top of a mountain driving up to the summit. There is nothing like watching the sun rise along the Blue Ridge Parkway.

Mother's Day starts the arrival of spring to the mountains. You can still expect frosty mornings, an occasional ice storms but off the mountain, nature is waking up from a long winter nap. Plan a hike along your favorite trail. It is usually too cold for the snakes yet, so any trail that boasts a lot of snakes is a safe bet for a Mother's Day wander. Beech Mountain Club and area restaurants offer Mother's Day brunches, churches offer services. One year, my boys told me they wanted to make me breakfast in bed for Mother's Day. They served me a piece of toast and Miller Lite. Boy did I feel pampered.

Memorial Day is when Beech Mountain officially opens for summer residents. The Resort opens for downhill mountain biking, the Beech Mountain Club pool, golf course and clubhouse open for business, and many local businesses throw open their doors breathing in the crisp mountain air. If you are a member of the Beech Mountain Club, the pool party for Memorial Weekend is a great affair. A snack shack opens for business offering not just food but your drinks of choice - hard core or soft. You can bring your own beverages to the pool. Just make sure they are cans, or in plastic cups. There's nothing better than getting some sun at the pool while listening to the lifeguards yell, "WALK" over and over again. The air temperature is still cool in May and June but the Beech Mountain Club pool is heated to a balmy 85 degrees. Many a day you'll see kids sitting in the pool with just their nose above the water, keeping the rest of their bodies warm.

Father's Day is another fun day at the club. A Father's Day brunch and dinner is offered to Beech Mountain Club members. Best part of the Beech Mountain Club Restaurant is the view. It sits on the side of a mountain. My family loves a little used table outside on the deck, where both the view and food are awesome (See Beech Mountain Club.) The tree right beside the table has a nice nest of bats, and it is fun watching them fly out at dusk.

4th of July is a fun holiday on the mountain. (See Roasting the Hog) Our personal hidden gem involves a picnic with adult beverages and a hike. We hike to the top of the mountain, watching the fireworks in several different places. Beech Mountain provides fireworks the Saturday before the 4th of July, so you may want to hike twice for both shows. One year it was so clear we counted 18 different firework displays in North Carolina, Virginia and Tennessee from the top of Beech Mountain, little bursts of color on the nighttime sky.

Labor Day is the official goodbye to the summer residents as the Beech Mountain Club pool closes for the season, and the Clubhouse moves into off season hours. The restaurant cuts back on the days it offers food finally closing for the season in mid October, except holidays.

Halloween on the mountain is quick and easy. Local businesses provide the candy for residents while a hay ride takes them around the mountain. My boys called this candy heist the "mother load" as businesses give out "real" and "big" candy bars along with bags full of other candy. The festivities end at Buckeye Recreation Center with a Halloween party, bonfire, Haunted Maze and games. If you want more of a "Trick or Treat" experience think about the Banner Elk Trunk or Treat in Tate Evans park for Halloween. Local residents and businesses open the trunk of their cars for Trunk or Treat, a haunted house is set up in the corner of the park along with live music and food. It's a fun event and a great way to show off those costumes to as many people as possible.

Thanksgiving on the mountain is when locals hold their breath waiting for opening day at Beech Mountain Resort. The resort aims for a day after Thanksgiving as opening day but all of this depends on Mother Nature. She's been kind to us several years in a row. Watch forecasts if you hope to ski

Thanksgiving weekend, as it may not be cold enough to make snow. (See snowmaking 101.) If you cannot hit the slopes that Saturday, Blowing Rock, and Banner Elk both hold Thanksgiving parades that weekend, complete with a visit from Santa Claus. Bring a bag with you to the parade as most of the floats enjoy throwing candy at spectators. I was once beaned in the forehead by a Smartie which my child then picked up and ate. Our first year at the parades, both boys were holding candy in their shirts and pockets as Mom failed in remembering their collection bags.

Which brings us back to Christmas, in a Winter Wonderland. If there isn't snow on the ground around your home, you can celebrate the white stuff at the Resort. (See Christmas)

31. YOU'RE STAYING HOW LONG?

Living on top of a mountain close to a ski resort brings many visitors through your home. I've learned the hard way that you cannot get all the day to day stuff of running a home while playing tour guide every day to visitors. In order to keep my day to day life less chaotic, my rule of thumb is playing tour guide every other day when I have visitors. Visitors don't understand that while we live in an amazing, beautiful place, we also have to work for a living and keep up with basic details of life.

If your visitors are winter visitors, I suggest sending a check list to them prior to their visit. I actually had a visitor from Florida who'd never seen snow! So, if they don't possess the winter necessities, many ski rental companies on the mountain rent bibs, jackets and other warm gear. I usually purchase on sale the small items - gloves, hats, scarves, toboggans, hand warmers, socks. I keep a nice stock of long underwear around the house because most will not squirm at the color pink, because no one sees your long underwear. I used to keep my children's old snow clothes, but gave up when space in my home became a priority. That and most children visiting were more into fashion, a pair of black bibs not on their priority list. One girl put on a pair of my collected snow pants, telling me she couldn't wear them because they had a rip in them. I looked everywhere, finally asking, "I don't see it."

She pointed to her knee, where there was the tiniest of rips, so small I had to put on my reading glasses to see it. As a mother of boys, I nodded saying, "Oh we can throw a piece of duck tape on that, honey."

She ran for her mother, who also put on her reading glasses, found the rip then stated, "Oh, she can't wear that. We'll go and purchase some new snow pants for her at the Resort." I wasn't going to mention the "tourism" prices, and that upon going back to Florida, she probably wasn't planning on wearing the pants to school, simply shrugging and letting it go. Remember with visitors, you can make suggestions. Just don't take it personally if they don't want to do your amazing, (been here longer than you ideas,) and go out on their own.

Once you get your visitors to the slopes, remember how invaluable a lesson or snow camp is. It frees up your time, and your children's time, not having to teach a life long hobby to someone else. If you have non snow enthusiasts, you can always light a fire, point out the tubing runs at the Resort, the sledding hill by Town Hall, the shops open in Beech Alpine Village and ice skating indicating that you, as host, are not obligated to sit with them at your home. We always make it clear that our morning plans include "first chair," meaning we're at the resort at 9am. Oh and to make it little more pleasant we always add in the "but make yourself at home."

Summertime visitors are different. Many already have a plan of attractions to visit - Linville Caverns, Mystery Hill, Tweetsie Railroad, while others are content with sitting in the woods and relaxing. I keep a drawer of brochures from all the local attractions, pulling that out, and letting them plan their day. If they are going to the pay attractions, there are a few I've already visited, not that I would pay to visit again. These are the days I can take care of the everyday life thing, letting them go out exploring.

I also keep several Blue Ridge Parkway Guides and Hiking Guides for visitors, including a pocket Hiking Guide. Here's a few titles that are a permanent fixture on my book shelf:

Hiking North Carolina: A Guide to Nearly 500 of North Carolina's Greatest Hiking Trails by Randy Johnson
Great Waterfalls of North Carolina by Neil Regan
Touring Western North Carolina Backroads by Carolyn Sakowski
Moonshine!; Recipes, Tall Tales, Drinking Songs, Historical Stuff, Knee-Slapper, How to Make It, How To Drink It, Pleasin' The Law, Recoverin' The Next Day by Matthew Rowley
Blue Ridge Parkway, North Carolina Ski Resort and Beech Mountain Books by Arcadia Publishing
Guide to the Blue Ridge Parkway by Frank Logue, Nicole Blouin and Victoria Logue
All the Field Guides to birds, mushrooms, weather, insects, mammals - children love looking through these.

Having these books available helps visitors plan out their vacation educating them on the mountain. I've found new tidbits of information in them for my own exploration, hence why this book will be a nice addition to your bookshelf. Hint! Hint!

Luckily for me, most of my family live too far away to visit the mountain, and those that love coming often are now renting or owning their own places. One friend that had a revolving door of visitors solved her problem. When someone mentioned they were coming for a visit, she'd say, "Great! There's a great little house here for rent, I'll call now and check availability." Sending out a message while still preserving their fun! Genius!

32. CAN'T WE ALL JUST GET ALONG?

Whether you are here for a visit or decide to live on Beech Mountain, friends make life easier. I have two types of friends, friends and close friends. Many friends are "fun hanging out with" friends, having some great food along with drinks. Close friends means having dinner with some pretty interesting conversations, and sharing a little more information about each other, because word travels fast around this small mountain town. Being in a small community like Beech Mountain, sometimes it is hard finding friends. Here's a few suggestions:

If you are simply here for a visit and needing a break from your flat mates at the cabin, several places on the mountain are great places for meeting new friends. On the snow, it is easy making friends on the lift (See things NOT to do on the lift.) You have about five minutes conversing with the person next to you, gauging their ability, finding out where they came from, possibly planning an apres ski meet at a local establishment. All it takes is stepping outside the box making first contact. I always tell my children that making eye contact when someone is speaking to you is a sign of respect, so look the person you are talking to in the eye, whether everyone is wearing mirrored goggles or not. It doesn't matter if they can see behind your sunglasses or goggles, they will notice you are looking at them. It does make a difference.

If you decide to live on the mountain, you can start meeting new friends by going to community events. You can always come across a crowd of locals at the Bark Park located in the Meadows by Town Hall, but some may think you are a stalker if you show up at the Bark Park without a dog. Don't worry, there are other places.

Signing up for exercise classes at Buckeye Recreation Center is a great way to meet people while staying fit on the mountain. You can visit their website for a calendar of available classes and other events. Buckeye Recreation Center offers free hiking classes during the summer months, and many local residents enjoy these trips. During the winter months, you can find some local snowshoe classes around Buckeye Recreation Center, and yes, if you do not have snowshoes they have some you can rent. If you ever want a workout that will make you wish you were dead, head up a mountain on snowshoes. Your butt will love you.

Residents find that the Beech Mountain Club is a great place to mingle. It can be on the golf course, of course, but you can also meet people in the dining room, having a bite at the Fairway Cafe, or even lounging by the pool in the summer months. Beech Mountain Club puts out a weekly bulletin during the summer months listing things to do on the mountain including lectures, classes, guided hikes, day trips and gourmet meal tastings. I always make reservations for two because someone will come out of the woodwork wanting to go with me making it a very pleasant event.

The local restaurants on the mountain offer different ways of meeting others. You can hang at the bar enjoying the singles scene, or sit outside listening to music. Most weekends on the mountain there will be some type of live music event, a great way of hanging out, meeting a few new friends and who knows, showing off those dance moves. Finally, if you are a winter visitor and have children, the snow camps are a great way to meet other parents. Your children will find a bestie during their time in the camp, and as an extension of them you will now have parents' friends on the mountain.

There is nothing better than having your children occupied with a friend's children while you sit drinking coffee or something a little stronger, with adult conversation.

Just remember that too many friends require time. Make your choices wisely and remember that the word "No" to a friend should not make them angry. Set your boundaries early. This is especially true for helping on the mountain. If you let yourself get dragged to every event you could suffer burnout. Pick your friends, pick your time wisely, and making decisions leading to a peaceful lifestyle.

33. THE BEECH MOUNTAIN LOVE STORY

They met in a bar, but what's wrong with that? I met my husband in a bar called The Horse You Came In On. The meeting was after a full day on the slopes, and a little apres ski afterwards.

They found that they had so much in common, a love of snow sports, hiking, general outdoors type people. They were around the same age, even listened to the same music as they got to know each other. They also found it pretty amazing that they knew many of the same people, further cementing that they were perfect for each other. They spent quite a bit of time with separate groups of friends explaining how this was meant to be, that serendipity happened!

"He's so gorgeous, and he doesn't care that I don't shave my legs for winter. He says up here on Beech Mountain, we do whatever it takes for extra warmth," she says to her friends with a smile.

"She told me she didn't care that I spend time with my friends, our time apart is a big component to a better relationship. Can you believe it?" He tells his buddies.

"Dang, you are lucky," one replies looking to his girlfriend cemented at his side.

They move closer together, a beautiful expression of love until something small happens. There is a whisper around the circle of friends, something said about one or the other. It could be true, but knowing the mountain probably isn't, unfortunately it is a small enough whisper that both begin to question the relationship.

"I swear, I think he is married to his friends more than me," she says dismally, texting him.

"Why can't she just hang with all of us, I feel stupid spending all that time with her girlfriends, all they talk about is how cold they are," he says to his friends looking back her way. He looks down to his phone, "Now she's texting me. She says she's sorry, she loves me and wants to get back together again."

He texts her back, they argue about what happens next, get back together, the love they felt in the beginning back in full force until,

She sees him talking with another girl.

Is this girl a friend? Probably. Does she believe that? Not really.

"I can't believe you would want to be with her over me, after I told you I loved you," she storms at him, her eyes flashing.

"What?" He asks looking around the bar for some help from his friends. They all sip their beers watching the show, enjoying the drama.

"If you can't be with only me, then we don't belong together." She says dramatically, her hand wiping a solitary tear from her eye. "We could have been perfect you know. We had something, but now you are dead to me." She bows her head in defeat, walking away.

He looks around the crowded bar before shrugging, heading back to his circle of friends. "I'm not exactly sure what happened," he mutters, looking over to her, she is busy talking to another guy.

A typical ski season love story, usually the events happen during one night in a bar.

34. VOLUNTEER OPPORTUNITIES ON BEECH

There are plenty of ways to give back to the Beech Mountain community. It can be as simple as picking up trash along your hike and depositing it where it belongs, to coming out with the community, showing support for events on the mountain. There are several major events on the mountain which call for all hands on deck in the form of volunteers.

Beech Mountain Metric, a classic Mountain Metric a 43 mile and 23 mile starting in Banner Elk and ends with a climb up Beech Mountain (everyone insert your groan here.) The event is completely managed by the people of the Town of Beech Mountain. Created after the famous Tour de Pont cycling rides, it boasts a hill climb that Lance Armstrong used to use when training for the Alps portion of the Tour de France. The end celebration of the ride is on top of the mountain. Volunteer opportunities include aid stations along the ride, SAG or aid cars trailing the riders, helping in any way they can, food volunteers for the end of ride celebration, and registration. You can contact the Town of Beech Mountain prior to the ride in the Spring adding your name for assistance.

Once winter thaws out on the mountain and the hint of spring hits the air, Buckeye Recreation Center and the Town of Beech Mountain hold open trail days. This is a great opportunity to meet other locals, get exercise and keep this beautiful place pristine. You can watch for trail days on the Town of Beech Mountain or Buckeye Recreation Center websites. Beech Mountain Resort holds trail days during the summer for the downhill mountain bike trails every Thursday. If you are a downhiller, make it a point to stop by, keeping these trails ready for working lift days, Fri-Sun.

WinterFest is a weeklong winter celebration at Beech Mountain Resort. This culminates at Winter Brewfest on the Resort in January. Volunteers can help check festival goers in, hand out glasses, check ID's, and cleaning up after the event.

"A Cool Five" is a road race run every June on the mountain (the temps are still cool then.) Running in the race is a challenge as it starts with a heavy uphill ending on a downhill. If you can't run you can also walk the course or hand out aid at stations, or managing the end of race celebration.

Downhill Mountain Bike Races on Beech Mountain, in the summer the mountain hosts down downhill races, and college mountain biking races. They need course volunteers handing out food and beverage at aid stations. Meet a few mountain bikers and seeing if they really are crazy to do the sport.

Mile High Kite Festival over Labor Day weekend is always in need of volunteers. Hand out free kites to children, serve food and drink, and try to keep everyone from running into each other on the Meadows. This is a wonderful event, the scenery of the kites spectacular, making you glad you are a volunteer.

Autumn At Oz is the fall festival where they open the Land of Oz theme park for a weekend (See Festivals.) This is the arrival of over 6K people touring this park and needs a slew of volunteers. The Chamber of Commerce is your first stop for information on how to help with this festival.

There's plenty of places to volunteer, and it is a great way to meet people on the mountain. Get out there and help out a little bit, it does go a long way.

35. PLAN B, or C, or D AND IN SOME CASES X!

We talked about mountain time, how everything slows down as the altitude changes. Another standard on Beech Mountain is adopting Plan B, or the art of flexibility. Nothing ever goes as planned.

One major factor is the weather, usually mother nature has a good laugh when Beech Mountain plans activities. Low lying clouds tease us as we wait anxiously for a fireworks display, fog and rain laugh in our face as we race on the roads of the mountain. If there is an event planned, Mother Nature usually puts her exclamation point on it.

Autumn at Oz is a wonderful event for the family, but Mother Nature likes to make a point. When it used to be schedule in October, it was not surprising to find it snowing, I've been there when is was snizzling, a combination of snow and drizzle, and I've been up there for the beautiful bluebird day. Still plan for all alternatives on a September day.

Summers on the mountain always mean bringing a jacket because Mother Nature loves the rain and often adds a little cold, making an afternoon in July feel like Fall in any other part of the state. I keep at least one raincoat and one jacket in my car at all times. I don't worry about umbrellas because I'm not made of sugar. I won't melt.

Visiting Beech Mountain and your plan is a nice evening out? Plan early. Most establishments close early on the mountain. There is no "Let's go out and grab a bite to eat at 10pm" here. Late night menus eaters usually end up in Banner Elk, if they don't have Lowlandophobia.

Most events will attempt an on time departure but remember, volunteers and staff sometimes are on mountain time. Be patient, it will happen, it just may take a little while.

Your car will never be clean. Winter is snow and gravel. Summer is rain and mud and gravel. When visiting the automatic car wash, always choose the under carriage wash regardless of the season. It keeps salt and muck and gravel from rusting out the bottom of your car. Your car will thank you.

If you haven't seen it in a day, beware! It will smell. It could be that ski mask someone "borrowed" without your knowledge, breathing their salmon breath in it all day, then casually sliding it back into your stuff. If could be your gloves that ended up wet on the inside gaining some type of funk you cannot describe, funk transferred to your hands when you wear them the next day. Worst yet is the towel the child casually left on the floor, used once, but "footed" by the moisture of the mountain. You can dare yourself the "smell" test but I've had too many items bring me to my knees after the "smell test" so I err on the side of caution, I just wash it again.

Hopefully you won't need this plan S but here's the mixture to remove skunk from an animal or human. Equal parts Dawn@ Dishwashing Detergent, Hydrogen Peroxide and Baking Soda. Soak in the mixture, lathering well, watching the eyes, and let sit for 5 minutes, rinse and repeat. If you're the one soaking, add a nice glass of wine, it helps. Hopefully you won't be Googling this at 6am as I did one morning.

Include in A-Z plans those people on "mountain time," the weather, and of course waiting in your car as the bear crosses the road, dragging the trash can behind him.

Face it, life would be boring if everything went along with Plan A, now wouldn't it?

36. WHY

"The mountains are calling and I must go," -John Muir

There are many reasons why people choose a mountaintop as their home. Beech Mountain is not different. There are different reasons for different people.

Some are escaping, escaping the crowds of the city, the push of traffic, the haze of pollution. They are seeking a simpler life where a traffic jam consists of 3 cars and a skunk, where coffee on a back deck while watching the fog roll through is considered the best part of your day.

Others try to escape an earlier life. There are stories on the mountain of people who come up here because they want to disappear. They are hiding from someone or something. Perhaps they stay on Beech Mountain because we are all friends on the mountain, where everyone starts fresh when they arrive. We don't ask much about the past because life begins at 5506 feet.

Others come for the sports, knowing that in a mountain town, they will find kinsmen with a love of the outdoors. Conversations are mainly about new snow gear at the start of ski season, or specific fishing spots, spoken with a promise not telling a tourist, and sharing pictures taken on the most recent hike.

Everyone is friendly on the mountain. It could be that cooler air keeps tempers down. It could be the beauty of a morning sunrise on a cold winter day making you feel wonderful. Or it could be when you are on the mountain you slow down. Your perspectives change when you take the time to look and appreciate what is in front of you.

I came to the mountain as a tourist, spending weekends for 6 years, grieving each time I returned home, where the temperature warmed, things sped up, and kids sat inside the house rather than roaming the woods. It took some convincing, but when you want something bad enough you are determined. My first year permanently living on a mountaintop was an adjustment, and I say that with a smile on my face.

I am here because this is where I belong, this is where I find my creativity, this is where I can walk in the woods, deer do not run away as I pass them. This place makes me laugh, it makes me sigh, it frustrates me.

But I wouldn't be anywhere else.

There.....look, now I let your coffee get cold. Let's warm those mugs up. We's all family on the mountain.

37. NOT SURE ABOUT BEECH MOUNTAIN? LET US TELL YOU WHY!

"Beech Mountain Club brought me to the mountain for an interview in October, along with my wife, Dara. She enjoyed touring the mountain while I went through 3 hours of interviews with different board members. I sat in the old dining room, now the bar of the club looking out on the view for 3 hours. I fell in love with that view and the mountain that day, moving here after getting the job." - Brian Barnes, General Manager, Beech Mountain Club

"I started skiing here in my younger days. I was at an age where I could go anywhere, I could go to the "bigger" mountains out west if I wanted. But, being able to enjoy 4 different seasons here, and seeing views that change on a day by day basis made me stay on Beech Mountain. Funny how I used to talk about 'Old Timers' on the mountain and now I am one of those 'Old Timers.' I still visit out west but this is where I live." - Gil Adams, Director of Ski Patrol.

"I came here as a kid, and now I bring my kids here. This is our Home Mountain." - Kevin Mullins, Stoplight Roundhouse Shawneehaw Slope

"Beech Mountain has a certain magic, you either feel it or your don't. Sure we go out west for our ski vacations, but this is where we call home." Sarah Mullins, Ski Patrol

"I remember getting a phone call with a Southern Accent asking me about joining ski patrol in North Carolina. I thought that was strange, skiing in North Carolina? Then I moved to Hickory, finding out you do ski in North Carolina and became part of ski patrol. I've been on Beech Mountain Ski Patrol since 1978. Shirley says we live up here because no one gets her off the mountain on a hot summer day!" Pete Chamberlin, unofficial Mayor of Christie Way.

"I was offered a job with a place to stay. I stayed for the snow! Plus the people are really nice!" Charlie Frisbe, Beech Mountain Recycling Center.

"Vicki had enough of the Florida heat, informing me she was moving from Florida to North Carolina, and after 28 years of marriage I figured I'd better follow her. Now we couldn't imagine living anywhere else, you can't beat the seasons on the mountain, especially the cool summer days," Famous Fast Eddie Plante

"My wife and I knew retirement wasn't part of our plan. We decided our best bet was living where we wanted to retire, and here we are." Bernie Knepka, President, Chamber of Commerce.

38. MANY THANKS!

Many thanks to all the characters on this mountain helping with suggested edits, hilarious stories (some too crazy to recount in this book) and their time reading the beta copy of this manuscript.

Thanks to my family, allowing the craziness of writing this book. The long nights, the long conversations with myself, their lives as guinea pigs on the page. Their support taking this unconfident writer to opening the first case of books with my name as author. Especially Jeff, who doesn't begrudge me the time to be creative, he actually supports it, his only request that he not be the focal point of any said essay.

Thanks to all my beta readers, your comments, suggestions, criticism and especially the praise very needed. Rereading the praise in moments of doubt.

Thanks to my friends of Beech Mountain, Tammy, Kim, Kate, Bonnie, Sarah, Nicole who never turned down a, "Let's grab a beer, I've got something to run by you."

More friends of Beech Mountain, Josh and Michael, Cindy, giving me some more historical and factual details to the book.

My editor, who totally understand my creative craziness and how difficult it is getting bogged down by the details when you just want to create. You make me look good.

Beech Mountain, the mountain where I find creativity, peace and of course too many good stories to recount. Perhaps a book two?

Of course, the greatest glory goes to God. I am so thankful for my talent, for the people you've place in my life and for the extraordinary adventures yet to come!

39. POSTSCRIPT

Remember that local legend showing up for a party at the WRONG house? How "we's all family on the mountain?"

A guy walks into a bar, saying, "You'll never guess…."

My beer is halfway to my lips, I pause asking, "What?"

"I did it again."

"What?"

"Yep, I was running late to a funeral in Banner Elk of a friend. Since I missed the service, I figured I'd show up at the graveside service. Pulling into the cemetery, I found the group, quickly getting out and quietly walking up to the service, already in session."

"So?" I ask with bated breath.

"Well, I stood listening, then started looking around, finally thinking, 'Who are all these people?' I was at the wrong funeral!" He said, laughing.

"What did you do?"

"Well, I stayed and said a prayer for the poor soul. Rest In Peace."

Remember, "We's all family on this mountain."

40. FOR MORE INFORMATION

Beech Mountain - www.townofbeechmountain.com

beechmtn.com

hikebeechmtn.com

Beech Mountain Resort

beechmountainresort.com

Chamber of Commerce

beechmountainchamber.com

ABOUT THE AUTHOR

Kelly Melang grew up in Ellicott City, Maryland. Working for the airlines, Kelly and her husband Jeff lived in many cities, including Boston, Cleveland and Baltimore before moving to North Carolina. The family lives in Beech Mountain, North Carolina with their two children, Wolfgang and Max along with a cute little rescue dog named Shawnee Haw.

Kelly's writing career includes local magazines. Kelly also writes for e-zines and blogs for businesses on the Internet, as well as writing copy. She also helps businesses manage social media accounts. She has written 7 novels with the first one due out in 2018.

An avid athlete, Kelly has finished marathons and triathlons, including several Half Ironmans. As a certified yoga teacher, she challenges her students through various classes.

This collection of stories started with a notebook on a beach in Ocean City, MD. There are still many stories swimming around Kelly's head. You can follow her blog www.blueridgerv.blogspot.com or her Facebook Fanpage www.facebook.com/ThatGreyArea

Kelly Melang's book, Views From 5506 A Guide to Vacationing or Living on Beech Mountain is available through Amazon. The book is a collection of humorous essays about life on a mountain top.

The Melang family loves being outdoors – they enjoy hiking, biking, skiing, and snowboarding. Following her family's motto, "Discover Life," Kelly enjoys living life to its fullest.

Made in United States
Orlando, FL
14 May 2023

33124147R20080